I0879085

Wonderful

Wonderful

Benoit Cohen

POINTED LEAF
PRESS

To Nonno,

"To those we love, we stopped talking, and this isn't silence."—René Char

FOREWORD
UZODINMA IWEALA

We all know that death—our death, the deaths of people we love—is inevitable. Through the ages we have asked and tried to answer what it means to die. In ancient societies there was—it seemed—more proximity to and thus more practical consideration of the process of leaving this world. In our modern era, in places with the resources to practice the cutting-edge medicine that can save or prolong a dramatically endangered life, sometimes it seems for the sole purpose of prolonging it, we find it so difficult to ask the question about how we want to die, what it means to choose the way you leave this world, or what it means to make that choice for another person.

Such is the place to which Benoit Cohen takes us in his destabilizing and moving account of his experience watching his own father battle and eventually die from pancreatic cancer. Benoit, at the same age I am now, with parents roughly the same age (if not a little younger) that my own parents are now, moved suddenly from all the time in the world with his father, to trying his best to understand all of the decisions around how a person leaves, not just life, but all the lives connected to that life, those passions, melancholies and joys, the wife, children, brothers, sisters, grandchildren, and more that make up the totality of a person's life and the essence of all we hold dear. How do you exit all of this with the dignity we have come to believe is an irrevocable right of human existence? What does it mean to choose not to suffer and why do we find it so hard to contemplate this choice? If you know a loved one is going to die, is it wrong to hasten their exit so they don't have to linger in pain or the fear that accompanies this ultimate loss? Is it immoral, if death is inevitable, to call that death quicker for yourself, for someone else, for someone you love dearly? Benoit doesn't know, but not knowing is not an excuse for not choosing a course of action when presented with that choice as the oldest son and person responsible for his father's well-being at the end of his life. His book takes us through the emotional considerations of these questions and the possible answers so we may not only consider, but also feel the pain of uncertainty or the quest for closure that may never come.

It is a testament to him as a human, as a director, and as a writer that Benoit invites us to journey through the space of control he is used to inhabiting as the author of numerous books and director of many successful films, and into a space of unknowing with all of the attendant emotional confusion this entails. His new work *Wonderful* has as its title a word I have only heard Nigerians use in its true sense, not as the glib synonym for "amazing," but as the devastatingly accurate "full of wonder," that suspended state where you are forced to see all facets of the surrounding world and maybe the world beyond. *Wonderful* is not just a book, it is an entire family's meditation on death, on the deaths of those they love dearly, the deaths of people they simply know (or possibly even don't), on the deaths that we will all have to face, one day, some day.

We are born without dignity, unaware even of the concept, naked and covered in some combination of our own and our poor mothers' fluids, screaming for dear life at the life now surrounding us as meaning-making for this new world starts and then continues and continues and continues. But neither those dying nor those watching them die want to contemplate a process of dying so ferocious as the birth that brought us into the world. We need and want our death to be instant. We need to have a sense of control, authorship, of direction. We need this, but this natural world needs nothing of the sort from us or for us. This gap is between what we want and what the world has in store for us. We are left to stare into it, full of wonder, until one day we are called to cross it.

Benoit's *Wonderful* takes us all the way to that edge to ask, "What would you do? What would you choose for someone you love and ultimately for yourself?"

UZODINMA IWEALA is an award-winning writer and medical doctor. He is a fellow at the Käte Hamburger Center for Apocalyptic and Post-Apocalyptic Studies at the University of Heidelberg, Germany. He lives in Brooklyn, New York and Heidelberg, Germany.

BENOIT COHEN

PROLOGUE

I sit before them. Law and order.

She's a judge. Him, a cop.

I tell them the story. Nine months and 27 days. Before, a life. After, death. In between, an interlude. A free fall.

They listen silently. I hold nothing back, spare no detail. They need to know. So I can know.

Occasionally, she winces. He sighs. Twice. "Any regrets?" the judge asks.

"None."

My story takes me back ten years. I pause, overwhelmed with emotion. I've told it all. They stare at me and exchange a furtive look.

"What you've told us is considered murder in the eyes of the law," the judge says, her voice neutral.

"First-degree murder," the cop specifies. "Because it was premeditated. And more importantly, it involved conspiracy to murder. Which makes it one of the highest crimes in France, along with genocide and crimes against humanity. A crime that is punishable by the heaviest sentences."

I laugh nervously.

"Sorry for being so blunt."

"Legally speaking, it's beyond the shadow of a doubt." "We're talking about patricide."

As I listen to them, the tone of their voices, the words they use, I feel like I'm on trial. Like I've come to the stand to tell my story after the plaintiffs and the rest of the family, and before the lawyers and prosecutor make their final statements. The judge sits before me. The public behind me. The jury to my right. But tonight, it's just the three of us. At the dining room table in a Parisian apartment, sipping red wine. The cop is a childhood friend. The judge, his wife of ten years.

Her daily life consists of rapes, robberies, murders and drug trafficking.

He started in narcotics and has moved on to the criminal police. He calls himself a leftist cop, "an old dude who's been beaten down by life."

"What's at risk?"

"If you go public with your story, you could be tried and convicted."

"But you probably won't get a harsh sentence. Definitely not life, which is usually given for this sort of crime. It's a special case."

"But there's a chance I'll wind up in jail?" They nod in unison.

I've never been in a courtroom. In a jail, yes. As a visitor. At the time, I was doing research for a screenplay. I spent two days in a detention center in western France. I remember a nagging feeling of claustrophobia. My personal freedom was taken away. I wasn't allowed to walk around in the corridors. I was confined to an office with bars on the windows. No contact with the outside world. At the mercy of my guards. My phone had been taken away. It was suffocating. Impossible to imagine several weeks, months, or even years locked up like that. But it was never a question. I was born on the right side of the tracks. I belong to the kind of people who don't get put in jail. "Good people," as they say. People who respect the law and whom the law respects.

"What you did is illegal," my friend continues. "But that doesn't mean you have to keep quiet. Everyone acts in keeping with their convictions. Even me, as a cop, I've done things against the law according to my beliefs. I knew I was taking a risk, but it didn't stop me."

"I didn't know what I did was illegal. I did what needed to be done."

"That doesn't change anything. If there's an investigation, you'll be arrested. But as a man, and as a son, you'll hold your head high."

His wife gets up and fetches a legal reference book from the bookcase. She flips through it quickly and pauses.

"Hold on, when exactly was the murder committed?" I shudder.

"Sorry. When did your father die?" "September 2010."

"Good news! The law only changed in 2017. The statute of limitations was ten years when it happened. And laws are only applicable from the moment they're passed. They aren't retroactive."

She smiles.

"You're free to tell the whole story."

I

THE ANNOUNCEMENT

Tonight, it's party time.

It's the grand opening of my new production offices. My two partners and I are setting up shop in a space connected to my home. White walls, black industrial windows, grey cement floor.

A few notable figures from the French film industry cluster around the buffet. We drink champagne, talk loudly, share our news, our most recent triumphs. We gloss over our failures.

The party is in full swing when my phone buzzes in my pocket. It's my mother. I step out into the courtyard to answer. Her voice is toneless as she announces that my father has just been diagnosed with pancreatic cancer. I say, "No." I say, "It can't be." I say, "Oh, shit." I say, "You want me to come?" She says, "I'm going to try to get some sleep." I say, "I'll come by tomorrow." She cries. Me, too. I hang up. Motionless in the middle of the courtyard, I think, my father is sixty-eight. I think of his fear of dying. How will he ever get through this ordeal? And my mother. How will she live without him? He's not dead yet, I think.

I think, he won't die. Not now. And my brothers? I need to call them. Later. I close my eyes. Take a deep breath. I wipe my tears with the back of my sleeve. I peer through the window at the guests. Fragility and tragedy have no business here. I muster my courage. Go back inside the office and head to the buffet. I pour a glass of vodka and shoot it. Return outside. I cross the courtyard, enter my home and collapse onto my bed.

As I drift off, I think of the world before. A happy childhood, loving parents, close brothers. The teenage years were tricky at times but never unhappy. A full adult life. An inspiring wife, cheerful children. I've been lucky.

During my early years, my parents never mentioned death. Especially my father. Talking about death—his or others'—would have brought bad luck.

The only exception: my maternal grandmother. I was nine years old. She was half a century older. When my mother told me the news, I remember bursting into uncontrollable laughter, followed by a slap. The only time I got smacked as a kid. How could I know that the breast cancer that had recently claimed my grandma was going to become a family curse? Soon I would watch an entire segment of my family die. My grandmother's twin sister, their brother, then four of my aunts, all victims of the same disease.

At home, we didn't talk about it. Silence made the unbearable bearable. We kept death at bay. Not naming it protected us. Not recognizing it made us untouchable. A few years later, my American uncle, the youngest sibling, suggested that all the women in the family, no matter what their age, take a DNA test to find out which of them carried the inherited BRCA1 mutation. My mother was the only one of her six sisters who didn't carry the killer gene. Our invulnerability was confirmed. Fate had built a fortress on our left side.

With the news of my father's cancer, the right side was hit. The structure was suddenly on the verge of collapse.

*

The next morning, I meet my mother in a café. Her face is pale, her features drawn. I imagine a restless night. I slept like a log, knocked out by the booze. When I woke up, my first thought was, "I need to be strong." As the eldest, I've often shouldered more responsibility than my brothers. Still, it was my father who steered the ship. He took care of family business: an old-fashioned patriarch, extremely benevolent yet omnipresent. Whenever a problem arose, if ever there was a conflict or decision to make, we turned to him. He took on his role of advisor, referee, and mediator with natural authority. His illness is going to be a game changer.

My mother sits across from me, sipping her espresso with foamed milk.

"Your father felt nauseated for days. His skin looked yellowish as well. We'd had oysters that week. He was sick the following day. He figured he'd eaten a bad one and that it would pass. But he kept throwing up. Finally, he went to the doctor, who ordered a blood test."

My father had gone to his brother's medical lab. Two extremely anxious men sitting across from each other in an office. Few words were exchanged. The results came in that night. An abnormally elevated level of gamma GT for an occasional drinker like my father. A scan was scheduled for the week to come.

On D-Day, my father insisted on going to the hospital alone. My mother went to lunch with a friend. She called him as she left the restaurant.

"Well?"

"Let's meet at home."

On the way back, my father called his brother.

"Did you know when you got the results?"

"Yes."

"Why didn't you say anything?"

"I couldn't."

When my mother got home, my father was standing far back in the dim living room. Fixing a lampshade. When he heard footsteps on the parquet, he turned and cracked a crooked smile. His eyes said, "I'm sorry." She walked over to him without a word. He took her in his arms. They cried.

*

I know I shouldn't. I can't resist.

I go online.

I want to know what lies ahead.

"Pancreatic cancer is the deadliest type of cancer. . . . It is usually discovered at an advanced stage. . . . Often too late to operate. . . . Remission is unlikely. . . . There's a five-year survival rate of 5 percent. . . . The illness progresses quickly."

I knew I shouldn't have.

*

First appointment at the hospital. The whole family is there: my father, mother, two brothers, and me. The surgeon sits across the desk, a manila folder in front of him. He offers a glimmer of hope: it's possible to operate. Suddenly, the survival rate jumps from 5 percent to 20 percent.

My father is devastated and asks no questions. My mother takes charge.

"The tumor is located in the head of the pancreas," the doctor explains. "Which is better. It blocks the bile duct, which quickly brings on icterus, in other words, jaundice. It means the cancer is diagnosed earlier. In other locations, symptoms develop later and often include stomach pain, which generally means the cancer has spread outside the pancreas. That's why it's usually said that cancer in the head of the pancreas is less serious. Nevertheless, I won't deny that it remains extremely serious. We need to operate as soon as possible."

He checks his schedule and proposes a date in ten days. After the holidays.

As we leave his office, I ask the surgeon about his rather unusual last name.

"You have the same name as a producer I worked with on a TV series."

"That's my brother," he smiles. Good sign. Obviously.

He gives me his cell number.

*

Christmas Eve. The family puts on a brave face. Seated at the big table in the dining room, I observe my father. He looks pale but happy to be surrounded by his wife, sister, sons, daughters-in-law, and seven grandchildren. My mother has fixed his favorite dish: rabbit stew with olives. We get drunk on champagne and laugh a lot, like usual. Everyone goes to great lengths to keep up appearances, despite the nagging question polluting our thoughts: “Is this our last Christmas together?”

After dinner, we head to the living room. It’s time for presents. Surrounded by socks, books and game consoles, my brothers and I give my father his present. A trip to South Africa for the World Cup the following summer with his three sons. Soccer is his passion. My father chokes back tears. But June is still a long way away.

THE OPERATION

We go with my father to the hospital the day before the operation. My mother, no stranger to the depressing atmosphere of hospital rooms, has tried to brighten things up. She's brought two travel bags packed with an array of items. She makes herself at home. She sets up a handsome, stylish lamp at the side of my father's bed, plugs in his clock radio, puts his crosswords and a pack of anise biscotti on the nightstand, changes the pillowcase, drapes an alpaca blanket over his lap, and hangs framed family photos on the salmon-pink walls of the room.

My father, in bed, watches silently in a daze. My brothers and I stand on either side of his bed trying to lighten the atmosphere. We recap the weekend's soccer games while our mother transforms the room into a four-star suite. We make fun of her aesthetic mania when she heads into the bathroom to replace the drab hand towels with fluffy charcoal-grey bath towels.

We head off with a lighthearted "see you tomorrow," making no allusion to the complex operation with an uncertain outcome that awaits.

As we step out of the elevator, we see people in white coats and patients looking worse for the wear. Some hobble along; others drag IVs on wheels. We force ourselves to keep up our trivial banter. We're in good health. Our father will soon be out of here. But suddenly as we step into the main lobby, we come face to face with a bald child in a wheelchair pushed by her father. She smiles at us and then disappears down a corridor. We're struck dumb by the image. We continue making our way to the entrance. The guard eyes us but stays mum. How many orphan-to-be sons or widow-to-be wives has he watched walk through here since the day started?

*

Operation day. No news that morning.
My mother calls the hospital every hour. She is repeatedly told that my father is still in the operating room. No other information. In the middle of the afternoon, a nurse tells her that, after six hours under the knife, her husband is finally in recovery.

*

That evening, my mother, brothers, and I go to the hospital.
Our father is too weak to have visitors.
The surgeon meets with the four of us in his office. We hear the verdict.
"It was a long and complicated operation, but I was able to remove the entire tumor. He'll now need chemotherapy to kill the residual cancer cells. He'll have regular checkups throughout the process to gauge the cancer's growth. If the treatment is effective and there's no relapse within the next five years, we'll consider him in long-term remission. On the other hand, if he has a relapse, there'll be no hope."
I latch on to the idea that everything went well and remission is possible, forcing myself to ignore the depressing statistics I found on the internet.
The worst is behind us.
A decade later, researching details for my book, I visit the same surgeon in the Paris suburbs where he now works.
"We try to be positive since a patient's morale plays a major role in the evolution of their disease. In France, we don't lie, but we don't tell the whole truth either. It's cruel to burden people with information they don't want to hear. In English-speaking countries, doctors are more direct. 'Sir, you have cancer. You have six months to live.' Less hypocritical, but extremely harsh."
He tells me about the two years he recently spent at a prestigious New York hospital. A ridiculous salary and unimaginable resources, but endless pressure. A brutally unequal health system and the constant threat of

litigation. The institution paid up to $400,000 in insurance to protect some doctors against lawsuits.

He pulls out my father's file. Now he can tell me more.

"Pancreaticoduodenectomy is one of the most difficult operations in modern surgery. The pancreas is a complicated organ because it lies deep in the abdomen. It is shaped like a long pinecone, divided into three parts: the tail, body, and head. Its location between the duodenum, stomach, and liver makes the operation extremely dangerous. When removing the head of the pancreas, the duodenum, essential to digestion, must also be removed. They can't be separated. The bile duct, stomach, pancreas and intestine are severed. Afterward they must be rebuilt by suturing the different organs to reconstruct the digestive tract. Which is why the operation lasts so long."

I tell him my uncle just died from the same type of cancer, and that my aunt also has growths on her pancreas. He suggests that my brothers and I get a DNA test, referring us to one of his colleagues.

The day of the appointment, my youngest brother is anxious about what he might learn and bails. To "lighten things up," we send him a photo of the funeral home across the street from the hospital's main entrance. Dark humor to deal with anxiety. A family trait.

The doctor we see explains that, according to the interpretations of our results, my uncle's and my father's cancers are not genetically connected. As for my aunt, her issues are chronic and most often benign. We leave his office relieved.

My brother is late for an appointment and drops me off a few miles from home. As I walk the rest of the way, I start thinking about my own death. Will it happen at the same age as my father? That's in 20 years. Twenty years is tomorrow. Or will it be later? At the same age as my maternal grandfather? In 41 years? An additional lifetime. And what will I die of? I'm surrounded by illness, yet my mother doesn't carry the BRCA1 gene. My father's cancer isn't genetic either. And even though I eat too much, drink too much, and live in a polluted city environment, I don't smoke, I work out regularly, and . . . Lost in thought, I nearly get run over by a motorcycle racing by on the street.

*

A few days after the operation, we send a case of wine to the surgeon as a thank-you. We don't know what he likes, but figure that a surgeon, like in a Claude Sautet film, must drink Bordeaux and smoke a cigar before hitting the tennis courts.

My mother spends every day at my father's bedside. She busies herself with trying to lighten the hospital atmosphere as much as possible. She orders in his meals, carefully selecting his favorite dishes. She sprays her perfume around the room. And each day, she adds some new personal item to the decor. My brothers and I put in only brief appearances, trying not to tire him out.

The doctors prescribe morphine. He continues to be in pain.

They up the dose.

At night, a nurse asks my mother to leave the room. Exhausted, she doesn't put up a fight. We invite her to dinner. She declines. Exhausted.

In the middle of the night, her phone rings. She leaps up for it. It's my father.

"You have to come! They're at the window. They're trying to get in."

"Who? What are you talking about?" "Men. They're out there. They look huge." My mother checks her watch. It's 3 am "Come, come quick! Please!"

"Don't worry, darling. I'm on my way."

She throws on clothes and a coat and jumps into her car. She turns on the radio and listens to a late-night talk show. A woman is talking about her husband's illness. My mother turns it off.

She speeds through Paris, runs a few red lights, and merges onto the highway. She hesitates at the turnoff, not sure which exit to take. By the time she realizes she has taken the wrong one, it's too late. She drives through a maze of small suburban streets. Lost. The sidewalks are deserted, no one to ask for directions. She can't stop thinking of her husband, alone with his demons. A newspaper deliveryman finally points her in the right direction.

She parks in the vacant hospital lot and hurries into the grey concrete building. The lobby is deserted. The elevator is empty. There's not a single soul in the fourth-floor corridors. She gets to room 402. My father greets her with a cry. She comforts him. It's her, his wife, his love. She cradles him in her arms. He's drenched in sweat, trembling. They hug silently for a few minutes. He tells her about his visitors: dark, hostile, ominous figures. She reassures him softly. It's over now. She's there. They won't be back. She's never seen him so frightened. She thinks of death. His relationship to death. His fear of death. Of human terror in the face of death.

She holds his hand. He falls asleep.

Outside, the sun has come up.

A nurse enters the room.

"What are you doing here?" he snaps at my mother. "My husband called for help. The morphine is giving him terrible hallucinations."

"That happens. We'll adjust his dose. You can't stay. Visiting hours start at 1pm. Come back then if you like, but you have to leave now. We'll take care of him."

When my mother returns that afternoon, my father tells her that after she left, the nurse lectured him like a child. He's not allowed to call his wife in the middle of the night. My mother is furious. She storms out of his room and into an office nearby to give the first person she sees a piece of her mind.

"Who do you think you are?" the head nurse barks. "His wife."

"If everyone acted like you, this wouldn't be a hospital anymore, it'd be a circus."

"Cunt," my mother mutters under her breath and disappears down the corridor. There is no way she is leaving her husband one more night in this place.

She calls me. She wants me to talk to the surgeon. How long does he plan to keep my father? I get him on his cell. He says that my father's condition is satisfactory and he could almost go home, but he'd rather keep him a while longer for observation. That's all my mother needs to hear to orchestrate a commando-style exfiltration. It's my job to track down a wheelchair while she contacts our physician, a GP and family friend who has been our doctor since we were kids. She tells him my father is coming home that night. We're going to need his help.

An hour later, my mother and I enter the hospital equipped with a rented wheelchair. We creep inconspicuously to the elevators. No one pays us any attention. We reach my father's room having carefully avoided crossing paths with any doctors or nurses. We get him dressed. He's over the moon, like a little kid up to no good. My mother gathers her things—the towels, pillowcase, and alpaca throw—while I collect photos scattered here and there. We help the patient into the wheelchair and make a beeline for the exit.

In the hospital parking lot, I load my father into the passenger seat, stealing worried glances over my shoulder. No security guards in sight. My mother climbs in back. I get behind the wheel and drive off slowly. The fugitive is ecstatic.

As far as exfiltrations go, this isn't my mother's first. A few years earlier, when her youngest sister's uterine cancer had metastasized, the doctors wanted to operate to relieve her pain. She was given a life expectancy of three months. The night before the surgery, a Sunday, my mother talked to an oncologist friend who refuted her colleagues' conclusions. Instead she advised preoperative chemotherapy. My mother called the hospital to cancel her sister's procedure. They told her it was impossible. The surgeon had blocked out the time and there was no way to back out now. The next morning, my mother went to the hospital, physically prevented the orderlies from taking her sister into the operating room, and brought her home. My aunt lived six more years after this last-minute about-face.

Back home, my father has a new lease on life. He gets settled comfortably in bed. My mother fixes him lemon risotto. He's in heaven. He makes her swear to never take him back to the hospital.

My mother promises. She'll take care of him. His smile is back; he jokes about his weight.

"For 40 years I've been dieting, and all it took was a few hours of surgery to drop 20 pounds. Who can top that?"

*

My mother and father lived their lives together for fifty years: a half-century of passion and togetherness. She always loved his kindness, humor, and pragmatism. He adored her combativeness, *joie de vivre*, and skills in the kitchen. She was the creative; he was the executive. She dreamed up harebrained ideas, he made them happen. Always on equal footing. But the rules of the game had changed. All it took was jaundice, a medical scan, and an operation to completely turn their relationship upside-down.

At the time, my brothers and I weren't fully aware of the profound upheaval underway. We made ourselves present as much as possible, took turns with my father, tried to relieve my mother. But we had our own lives, professional obligations, and families to return to once our mission was accomplished.

My mother never got a break. She was there for him, tirelessly, often alone, sometimes with help. Visitors would ask about my father, they would feel sorry for, pamper, and spoil my father. She stood at his side, invisible. She served the sentence with him, minus the pain and prospect of death, but adding silence. Few people show concern for the caregiver. Yet being the spouse of someone who is sick is a full-time job, a total commitment. You can never let your guard down, you must always be up to the task, 24/7. A patient's remission depends on their morale, and their morale depends on you ensuring they want for nothing. That they suffer as little as possible, that they're never too hot or too cold. That their meals are tasty, easy to digest, not overly repetitive. That they sleep. And if they don't sleep, neither do you. Be happy you're in good health. You're lucky. He's not. The patient is often in a bad mood, can't stand the state he's in, is ashamed of what he's going through and what he's putting you through. Illness is humiliating. So he becomes irritable, even tyrannical at times. Yet he's allowed to. He's the one dying. Not you. There's no way you can complain. Or ask for anything in return. Sometimes you can't take it anymore. You want to drop everything. Run away. Scream at the patient that he's a pain in the ass. That you didn't sign up for this. That you aren't his mother, his nurse, or his dog.

*

Yesterday, I had lunch with my mother. She was in a good mood. She told me about her new ideas for decorating the house. When my father died, I figured she'd leave this place. Painfully replete with memories. I imagined she'd start over from scratch. But she stayed. She's taken care of this home they built together. She likes to live surrounded by memories. Every detail, each burnished sconce, every patched lampshade reminds her of him. Each morning when she turns on the cold tap in the bathroom and the water runs warm, she thinks of him. My father was friends with a plumber whose main shortcoming was installing the water pipes alongside the heat pipes.

"Your father is there every day when I wash my hands," she says. "It's the most fantastic thing he did to make himself eternal."

THE INTERLUDE

When he's recovered from his operation, my father heads to the eighth floor of the hospital to meet with his oncologist. He waits in the corridor. He doesn't want to sit with the patients in the waiting room. Especially doesn't want to be associated with the "sick patients." He's not one of them. He has nothing against them individually, but he can't stand what they represent. He keeps his distance. They're probably going to die. He is going to live.

The oncologist prescribes standard chemotherapy with gemcitabine. A 48-hour treatment every two weeks for six months. The goal is to kill any malignant cells lingering in his body. If the treatment goes well and there is no metastasis, we might imagine a brighter future.

My father negotiates for treatment at home. This special dispensation is very rare, but the doctor takes my father's hospital phobia into account, along with his extreme anxiety. She tailors a protocol specifically to him. My father was a gentle, altruistic man who used to obtain favors with his kindness and charm.

For the transfusions, he will need a catheter placed in the axillary artery above his heart. The peripheral veins are too fragile to handle the toxic drug. His will be an outpatient surgery under local anesthesia that will last about 45 minutes. No extra nights in the hospital.

The end of winter and beginning of spring are punctuated by my father's chemotherapy. Every two weeks, he goes to the oncology department. A one-and-one-quarter-inch bulb is taped to his chest and hooked up to the catheter, which releases the drug into his body over the course of several days. He always goes alone. And drives himself home afterward, listening to salsa music.

*

I remember my father sitting in an armchair in the living room waiting patiently for the liquid to filter into his bloodstream. He'd read the paper. Never a book. He wasn't a reader. He didn't go to the movies or the theater either. And museums, even less. His culture was life itself. And his family. He was not an erudite man, yet he was refined and had a keen sense of humor. He would proudly tell the story of how he failed his baccalaureate nine times. At that time in Tunisia you could take the exam three times a year. He liked to say he failed with "beach" honors. Next, he enrolled in the fine-arts school, following a girl he had a crush on. He never took the final exam. In those days, he earned a living as a bartender and a poker player, while his childhood friends pursued brilliant careers. My father had developed a sort of complex, but he was comfortable with not being an intellectual. He read the sports pages religiously each morning. He analyzed the sports news, particularly soccer. He knew all the players, journalists, sportscasters, tactics, transfers, predictions, rankings, schedules. His passion for sport was absolute. The explosion of cable channels broadcasting matches from all over the planet at any time of the day or night was a genuine revolution for him.

Soccer is my father. Family games on Sunday mornings in the woods outside of Paris. Wednesdays on television. Excursions to the stadium. His existence, and our childhood, was punctuated by soccer.

For every major international competition, he turned our living room into a sports bar. We'd invite about 20 people. It was fun, electric, euphoric when we won, dramatic when we lost.

I particularly remember the evening of July 2, 2000. France and Italy were facing off in the Euro Cup final. The room was packed, the sofas were lined up facing the big-screen television purchased especially for the World Cup that France had won two years earlier. A good-luck television. My father in the front row. Cheering at every opportunity. Cursing whenever the Italians would approach the French goal, guarded by Fabien Barthez. When the Italian team scored in the 55th minute, it was a shock. The minutes ticked by. Regulation time was over. A few additional seconds. The Italian fans were already on their feet singing their national anthem. One last opportunity and—miracle of miracles—France scored. An explosion of joy rocked the living room. A swell of jubilation from the city heard through the open windows. My father whoops in elation and embraces a friend. I come over to share in his excitement. His face is blue. He's stopped breathing, on the verge of passing out. The others, caught up in the jubilation, don't notice a thing. I sit him on the couch to help him catch his breath. He slowly recovers and lifts his fist in victory.

That night, I realized my father's mortality for the first time. Before this scare, he'd never been ill, never had an operation, never displayed any sign of weakness. He was solid as a rock. Outside of his passion for lemon ice cream, he had no addictions that I knew of. He didn't drink, didn't smoke, had never taken drugs. But at that moment, slumped on the couch gasping for breath, I pictured him dead.

As kids, my brothers and I never missed a game France's national team played at the Parc des Princes soccer stadium. We would go to the game like it was church. A friend of my uncle's who worked at the French Federation of Football would get us tickets. Always the same seats: Tribune J Blue.

We'd come out of the metro and merge into the throng flowing toward the stadium. The closer we got, the greater the tension, the more radiant my father. Some nights, he'd buy us scarves; others, a cap. It was time to party. Once we got past ticket inspection, we'd climb the stairs and sit on the plastic stadium seats. There were chants, banners, the national anthem, hot dogs at halftime. And above all, the pleasure of communing with my father. I loved sitting at his side and watching him during the games. He was ecstatic. He'd spend the entire game calling to the players, shouting instructions. Given the crowd noise and distance from the field, no one, other than our neighbors in the stands, could hear him. My brothers and I would make fun of him. Until the day when, during a lull in the spectator noise, he shouted, maybe louder than usual, "Rocheteau, break free on the left!" To our great surprise, the right forward of the French national team turned toward us and began running in the direction indicated by my father. Our hero.

At that time, like most boys of our generation, we collected Panini albums. We'd exchange stickers at school during recess. Michel Platini was our idol. We followed his exploits, in blue for the French national team, in green for Saint-Étienne. We dreamed of meeting him.

Our dream almost came true.

When my parents founded a children's clothing line and were beginning to open franchises around the country, Michel Platini contacted my father: he wanted to open a shop for his wife. He planned to come to our house in the country to finalize the deal. My brothers and I could not have been more excited. We had everything prepared: the albums, ready to be autographed; the goal, built out of three pieces of wood; and the ball, inflated at the town gas station. We could already picture "Platoche" shooting one of those free kicks he had such a knack for.

Then scandal struck.

Two days before our idol's visit, France's leading sports newspaper ran the headline "Broken Green." A two-page article revealed that one of Platini's teammates was having an affair with his wife. No more shop. No more autographs. No more free kicks. The dream was dead.

*

Another of my father's loves was a card game called *belote*—a passion cultivated with his Tunisian friends, from the beach of La Marsa to their shared exile in France.

There was always an excuse to play cards, especially in the summer. Not a single cocktail hour went by without a card game. As a teenager, I was happy to simply watch the adults. I was impressed and never would have dared join in, until the day when they were a player short. I was finally invited to sit at the table. Serious pressure, maximum concentration, making sure to count the trumps, play the right cards, not disappoint my father. The first round went well. We won. I was allowed to play again. I haven't stopped since.

In winter, we'd also play cards. Not as often but still regularly. On the days my brother's restaurant in southern Paris was closed, we got in the habit of organizing "couscous-*belote*" parties: we'd share the traditional North African dish with about thirty friends, happily breaking into tables of four afterward. My father took these evenings very seriously. He would unfailingly end up a finalist of games that would last well into the night.

During his treatment, we came up with a new concept: "chemo-*belote*." There were just four of us: my wife, an old family friend—who succumbed to cancer himself a few years later—my father, and me. We'd set up in my parents' living room, light a fire in the fireplace, and launch into endless games punctuated with therapeutic laughter.

On these rare occasions, my father was capable of unusual displays of tenderness. If he won, he'd give me a high five and a hug. These bonding moments were special. My father was an undemonstrative man who didn't share his feelings or emotions. Even with us, his children, he spoke little and displayed affection sparingly—a quick pat on the shoulder every once in a while for encouragement or comfort. A Jewish friend once told me how her mother, who'd been in the extermination camps, never kissed her. When she grew up, she reproached her mother's coldness and her mother replied, "I don't kiss you because that way, if we're ever separated, you won't miss it." Did my father's reticence come from a similar fear of separation or death?

For him, affection was displayed through a look, smile, or a rare tender word. Like many people of their generation, his parents never said

"I love you," and he inherited their restraint. For years, I had trouble telling my children I loved them. I was tender and affectionate but wouldn't put the feeling into words. It wasn't until they grew up and complained that I learned to voice it. My daughter was the first. She chided me for not expressing my love enough. I managed to wriggle out of the situation by making her laugh. More recently, my son. One day when I was dropping him off at the train station, he hugged me and said "I love you." "Me, too," was my reply. He called me on it. "How come fathers never tell their sons they love them?" I hugged him again and whispered "I love you" in his ear. He burst out laughing.

*

I miss my father's laugh. He had a dry wit that was disarming. Never malicious. He made fun of everyone. Without exception. From the first time they met, my mother was drawn to this part of him. She came from a family where no one ever laughed at someone else's expense. So she immediately went for this garrulous guy with a mischievous gleam in his eye.

I remember one summer when my American uncle invited my parents to spend a few days at the sea. But, to their great despair, my New York aunt never wanted to leave their hotel. She insisted on eating every meal in the air-conditioned hotel restaurant. One day, my parents begged off with the excuse of taking a romantic walk. They ate lunch in a tiny beach joint that served simple, delicious local fare. My aunt was intrigued and suggested the group return the next day. Once there, she decided to try everything. She ordered every dish on the menu, only eating a few bites of each one. The rest she fed to the stray dogs roaming the beach. When the waiter brought the dessert menu, my father intercepted it and handed it to the dogs.

That was his sense of humor.

His favorite target was my mother. He loved teasing her, and she would gladly volunteer. She was his best audience. I even suspect that, at times, she made herself an easy target so they could laugh together. My father also loved making fun of his brother, a superstitious, obsessive man who had a terrible time making decisions. Choosing what dish to order in a restaurant was an ordeal; buying a new pair of pants or watch was an arduous task. He would pore over market research to determine which was the best product to set his sights on. His neurosis hit a climax when it came to buying a bathroom mirror. He was simply incapable of deciding, leaving the wall over his sink bare for two decades. One day at a family reunion, my father quipped, "You better hurry or else, by the time you get that mirror up, you won't recognize yourself."

*

Chemotherapy saps my father's energy. He no longer leaves the house, except for an occasional meal.

His first major postoperation outing was the DVD release party for a documentary I made on a famous American author.

To celebrate the event, I managed to convince the maestro to travel from Los Angeles for a book signing at the concept store my parents had opened not long before then. My youngest brother catered a buffet. A long line formed in front of the writer, who signed his books with gusto. But across the vast lobby, my father, seated comfortably in an armchair, stole the show. Like Marlon Brando at his Long Island villa, Don Papa greeted his friends one by one. Had he held out his hand, they would have kissed it. Neither he nor they could imagine that, for most of them, that was the last time they'd ever see each other.

*

At the beginning of June, my father finishes his first chemotherapy. He's extremely fatigued but experiences few side effects. No nausea. No hair loss. No canker sores. No diarrhea. His treatment is scheduled to resume in the fall.

*

The FIFA World Cup has just begun and our trip to South Africa is coming up fast. The day before we leave, my father has a series of tests. The doctors need to evaluate the progression of his cancer after the first round of chemo.

My father doesn't want the results sent to the hotel. He'd rather enjoy this break. He'll worry about the rest later.

*

"Let's meet directly at the airport."

In the taxi, I think about the unprecedented escape ahead. This will be the first time we've ever spent time alone with our father, without our mother along.

Our family has always stuck together. I have very few memories of my parents apart. With the exception of the times my mother went with her sister to the south of France to design their new children's clothing collection. My brothers, who were still small, went along, while I stayed home alone with my father.

Every night, we'd eat at a pizzeria in the Latin Quarter. Egg and artichokes for him. Ham and mushrooms for me. Without fail. My father wouldn't say much. I was ten, too young; it was hard for him to create a connection. He was only interested in me later, when I became his friend. So I would talk for both of us. I'd tell him about my life at school. I'd go into detail about my teacher's eccentric outfits, lessons on Vercingetorix, whom

I particularly admired. I would share my first crushes, brag about my goalkeeping prowess at recess. I was so happy to have him all to myself. This ritual lasted a few years. Until the day I got sick. Raging fever and severe headache. My father had no experience with this sort of thing. He panicked and called his brother, a doctor and real worrier, who thought it could be meningitis. I was given a spinal tap. A needle pierced my backbone. I remember a terrifying crack, a shooting pain, and three days of paralysis. My worst childhood memory. My mother was furious at my father's lack of composure and never left me alone with him again.

Lost in thought, it takes me a moment to feel my phone vibrating in my jacket pocket.
I answer.
It's the surgeon.
He has the test results. It's not good.
The cancer has spread. It's terminal.
"How long?"
"A few months."
Sucker punch to the gut. I hang up.
The highway guardrail streams past.
"A few months." What does "a few months" mean? Two? Three? Four? Six? Maybe eight? Or twelve? A year. The time left to live.
I think about an article I read a few days ago. In November 1981, the French president François Mitterrand wrote to Anne Pingeot, the mother of his daughter, to announce his cancer. "Today I got sentenced in court. The death penalty has been reestablished." The doctors gave him between three months and two years to live. He died 15 years later.
Believe in miracles. It's all we have left.

Why didn't I rebel at that point? Why didn't I question the surgeon? We could have gotten a second opinion. Asked for more tests. The operation had gone well. The treatment also. My father seemed to be doing well.

And suddenly, this crushing blow. Could there have been an alternative? Maybe if he'd started another round of chemo right away, the cancer would have slowed? Those are questions I could have asked. Instead, all I said was "How long?"

We were about to embark on the experience of a lifetime, and I didn't want to ruin it.

The taxi pulls up outside Terminal 2G.

I get my luggage. Enter the airport. My father and brothers are already waiting at the check-in counter. They greet me with huge smiles.

"We're off!" my father chirps. "Go France!" my brother adds.

Six months ago, no one knew if my father would actually be able to make this trip. Now, here he is, on his feet, beaming. My brothers look radiant as well.

On the plane, I sit beside my youngest brother. I lean close.

"I got a call from the surgeon on the way to the airport."

"Nope. Nuh-uh. Don't wanna know. We'll worry about it later. For now, we're having fun."

I obey.

Later, at the hotel in Cape Town, I share a room with my other brother. Before we fall asleep, I try to confide.

"Please, let's just enjoy this. We'll talk about it when we get back, okay?"

I shut up.

I am the only one who knows, for sure, that this is our last trip, our last summer, our last World Cup.

*

Our stay in Cape Town is like a dream. We discover the city in a festive atmosphere, sample the local cuisine, spend our afternoons on the patios of bars watching the soccer games. We mingle with fans from Brazil,

Spain, and Japan. We also go to the stadium, twice. The first time to cheer on France against Uruguay, the second to see Italy play Paraguay. Two mediocre games that end in a tie. Doesn't matter. My father is so alive, incandescent. He walks, shouts, chants, savors every instant. My brothers as well.
Haunted by the surgeon's diagnosis, it's harder for me to stay in the present, but I put on a good show. I focus on my father's joy. Even if his life ended now, he will have experienced this moment of exuberance with his sons. Other times, when negative thoughts get the upper hand, when I tell myself that this makes no sense, he'll soon be dead, and all these memories will be reduced to ashes, I double the dose of mojitos.

More than once during the week, I surprise my middle brother lost in thought. Later on, he'll admit that he had already lost faith as well. The youngest, however, will remain hopeful to the end.

One afternoon, I find myself alone at the hotel bar with my father. We sip piña coladas on the terrace overlooking the ocean, watching the powerful waves crashing onto the rocks, feeling like we're at the edge of the world. He asks about my work. He has always been proud of me being a filmmaker, both intrigued and thrilled by a milieu he knows nothing about. This day, while the sun beats white on the sea, the temperature climbs, and my father's face is beaded with sweat, he talks to me as he never has before. He tells me what he loved about my films, what moved him in the stories I told, and even what bothered him. He asks about my projects. I go into detail about the plot, cast, and financing of the film I'm preparing to shoot. A film he'll never see.
Shortly after his death, I found a box of photos in one of his desk drawers. Advertising columns plastered with posters for my first feature film. Roughly 20 nearly identical snapshots. One would have been enough.
Today I'm filled with emotion when I look at these mementos. I imagine him walking up the Champs-Élysées with his analog camera around his

neck, immortalizing his son's establishment as a filmmaker. He allowed me to live this dream, despite his reluctance and doubts. When I chose to study architecture after high school, he was pleased. When I changed course a few years later, he was upset but didn't stop me. On the contrary. He supported me at a time when this new direction seemed out of reach. He shared this open-mindedness with my mother. They gave me the strength to push myself and reach for my dreams. To live the life I wanted. I am forever grateful to them.

We'd never spoken about any of this, like so many other things. Though I regret it now, I don't blame him. I should have instigated the discussion, like when my son told me he loved me. When my father was a boy, nobody expressed their feelings. As he grew older, he withdrew into this silence. Even his relationship with my mother, who unlike him has no trouble opening up, didn't change anything. We, his children, should have cornered him, questioned him about his past, gotten him to talk about his feelings, hopes, and dreams. But our discussions were limited to the details of daily life. The pursuit of happiness from day to day. We lived happily. But we didn't talk. Now it's too late.

*

When I think back on our trip to South Africa, I realize what an effort it must have been for my father to follow us from stadium to stadium, from restaurant to restaurant, from bar to bar. He put on a brave face. He hated when we asked him how he felt and if he was tired. He refused to be treated like a sick person. We all kept pretending. Denying the reality. That's the way he liked it. We were there to have a good time. Fun and nothing but fun 'til the very end.

The last day, we decided to summit Table Mountain, which overlooked Cape Town. We took a cable car and then continued on foot to the top, over 3,500 feet above sea level. Our father, on his last legs, gave up halfway. He leaned against a guardrail to rest. Smiling. I immortalized the moment on my phone. He's standing straight. His black duffel coat draped over his shoulders. In the background is the sprawling city and the ocean as far as the eye can see. He looks exhausted but serene. It's the last photo I have of him.

But not the best. It's slightly overexposed and the composition is bad, yet it's the most moving. It's pinned up over my desk, next to a portrait taken a few years earlier in which he's in fine form, sitting on the patio of a beach restaurant sucking on a toothpick. There's a hint of anxiety in his gentle gaze as he stares off into space. He wears a heather-grey T-shirt. His curly, salt-and-pepper hair is thinning. He has his life before him.

From that day on, I no longer photographed or filmed him. I chose to keep that final image. He is tired but alive. Climbing a mountain.

*

Back in Paris, my father announces he plans to rest up for another trip. This time with the whole family. His wife, sons, daughters-in-law, and seven grandchildren. He wouldn't miss it for the world: one week on the west coast of Italy, like every year for the past 30 years.

His grandparents, natives of Livorno, immigrated to Tunisia in the early twentieth century. My father was fluent in his ancestors' language. His whole life, he would take us to the country of his heart. Every summer, we'd spend a few weeks between Liguria and Tuscany.

Our vacations were punctuated by the voices of *Urlatori (Howlers of the Dock)*. Toto Cutugno, Riccardo Cocciante, Pupo, Eduardo De Crescenzo: singers who howled their desire and despair. Though such a private man, my father had a heartfelt passion for these tormented souls. He was crazy about their sappy declarations of love. "*Perché io da quella sera / Non ho fatto più l'amore senza te / E non me ne frega niente senza te.*" He knew their lyrics by heart. Each year, we piled into the car and drove south from Paris. Once we had passed through the first tunnels after the Nice exit, we waited to hit the Italian border, crank up the car radio, and start belting out at the top of our lungs. All the Italian pop classics, without fail. We sang ourselves hoarse until we arrived.

Our destination: a village on the coast south of Cinque Terre. Narrow streets, colorful buildings, a medieval castle, churches, and trattorias.

We split our time between the beach and a wooden motorboat we had rented on the harbor. We navigated along the coast and ventured all the way to the little islands in the gulf. After a swim in the crystal-clear water of one of the coves, we stopped at a restaurant built right on the rocks. We ate spaghetti alle vongole and fried calamari.

We watched the sailboats on the horizon. From time to time, a gigantic cargo ship as tall as a building crossed the bay, announcing its presence with great blasts of the horn. As the sun sank behind the castle turrets and the first diamonds glittered on the surface of the sea, we returned to the village. We had lemon ice at the port and sat on a bench along the shore to watch the passeggiata. An ancestral tradition of the promenade. My father could sit there for hours watching the elderly villagers, noisy families, and honeymooners amble by.

At nightfall, we also liked to take the winding road up to the top of the hill where a small hamlet clings to its side, a few houses built along the banks of a river that flows into the sea. "There is this river. One cannot tire of watching it. How beautiful are rivers, especially when they reach their end, enormous, like this one," Marguerite Duras wrote about this spot. We loved watching the fresh water flow into the salt water while sipping a local white. We'd savor grilled fish, lulled by the sound of celebrations on the opposite bank. Over the tops of the parasol pines, the marble quarries of Carrara looked like rugged snow-capped peaks.

Though we love the idea of sharing all this once more with our father, the doctors veto it: he needs to rest up in advance of his next round of chemo.

*

July already. I realize I haven't told anyone about the phone call with the surgeon on the way to the airport. My brothers don't seem to want to know. They didn't ask about it when we got back from South Africa.
I could tell my mother about it. I don't.
I could pick up my phone to get more details, a new diagnosis. I don't.
I latch onto the idea that, in order to fight, my father needs to be in the best mental state possible. That by respecting the silence he's imposed upon us, we're helping him be stronger. We need to put on an unwavering positive face. Hide our doubts.
And yet, I'm not fooled. No one is. So to keep from sinking into despair, I summon other resurrection stories. Like the one a French friend in New York told me a few weeks ago. She'd been diagnosed with aggressive terminal cancer at the age of sixty. She decided to sell her condo, get rid of all her possessions, and return to France with only a suitcase, to spend the rest of her life close to her family. In Paris, she was offered palliative chemotherapy. It wasn't going to cure her but it would improve her quality of life during her final weeks. To everyone's surprise, she began to improve. A few months later, the doctors told her she was in remission. She'd lost everything. She no longer had a house. Just a few clothes. But she was alive.
Believe in miracles. In the impossible. In pipe dreams.
In the things that only happen to other people.
As long as my father is here, as long as I can hear his voice, touch his skin, see his hands moving, hear him laugh, I want to believe.

*

While waiting for fall and a looming additional round of chemotherapy, my parents head to their country home in Aveyron, southern France. My mother introduced my father to this lush and rocky region where she spent part of her childhood. He immediately fell in love with the rugged

nature, fresh air, cows, and regional cuisine, the opposite of what he left behind in Tunisia. In the 1980s, they bought a farmhouse. An edifice with thick walls covered in flagstone. A sloped garden enclosed by low drystone walls. A few fruit trees. A spring. A large linden tree to offer shade in the summer. A home they spent ten years rebuilding.
My father always loved doing home improvement. He spent most of his free time, weekends, and vacations with a paintbrush, screwdriver, or hammer in his hand. It was the way he cleared his head. A remedy to his natural anxiety, a way of forgetting the financial difficulties linked to their business, always on the brink despite growing in its success. My father was a gambler. Always forging ahead, constantly reinvesting what he earned to launch a new project. That's what drove him. The cold sweats this produced were like a drug. Even in the most critical moments, he never let anything show. I grew up thinking we had money, but that wasn't always the case. Invariably the same idea: as long as we don't talk about it, it doesn't exist.

That summer, despite his fatigue, he spends his days painting the garden furniture. He repairs the damage from the snow last winter, sands the shutters, varnishes the chairs, descales the faucets. He forgets his illness.

Ten years later, when I think back to these few weeks of respite, I still wonder why I didn't visit him at the time. On July 23, he celebrated his 69th birthday alone with my mother. I knew the clock was ticking. Was it my way of cheating death? Refusing fate? There would still be dozens of walks in the fields surrounding the farmhouse. Hundreds more bike rides. Thousands of card games in the garden. An infinite number of occasions to sample local delicacies between fits of laughter. Yes, of course there'd be other summers . . .
Or did I simply need a break? For six months I'd been watching my father slowly decline. I think I needed this break to recharge my batteries. In anticipation of the difficult road ahead.

As the days go by, he grows increasingly tired. On August 20, as summer draws to a close and the first storms make their appearance, my father has an episode in which he feels unwell. The village doctor pays a house call. He advises my mother to return to Paris. The nearest hospital is 35 miles away. It's too big a risk.

When it's time to leave, my father makes his rounds of the house one last time. He checks that the shutters are closed, the water and power turned off. I imagine him standing alone in the cool, dim light of the living room. I think of an excerpt from *The Cherry Orchard*, a play by Anton Chekhov that he never read: "I'll sit just one minute longer. It's as if I never saw before what the walls in this house are like, what the ceilings are like, and now I gaze at them greedily, with such tender love. . . . Oh, my darling, my sweet beautiful orchard! . . . My life, my youth, my happiness, goodbye! . . . Goodbye!"

Once the luggage is loaded into the car, my mother offers to drive. My father refuses. He insists on driving. That's how it's always been. No reason to change now. Don't break habits. A form of resistance.

My father drives like a demon along the winding mountain roads on their way to the station. He breaks every speed limit. More than once, he nearly swerves off into the ravine. My mother is terrified but keeps her mouth shut. Perhaps it wouldn't be so bad to crash into a tree and die together, she thinks.

They arrive safe and sound at the station.

Once there, my father feverishly insists on buying the newspaper. My mother tries to talk him out of it but he sends her away. He hasn't read the sports page for two days! He heads off. Their departure time approaches. My mother starts to worry. She looks for her phone. Out of battery. Another passenger lends her his. It rings several times but no answer. Departure is imminent. My father suddenly reappears, drenched in sweat. My mother, torn between relief and anger, drags him to the train.

"You had me so scared!"

"Sorry," he replies, distressed.

They board the train. The doors close behind them. My father sleeps the whole way.
When they arrive, my mother holds him up with one hand and pushes the cart with the other. She apologizes and skips to the head of the line. They climb into a cab.

When they get home, my father collapses onto the bed.

He has one month left to live.

THE LIE

His father died of a heart attack, howling in terror.
In his family, fear of death and the passage of time is an old neurosis. When my father was a boy in Tunis, death was taboo. At the dinner table, my grandparents wouldn't allow their children to talk about those who'd died. When I became a father myself, I learned that when you don't speak to children about death, they often develop an apprehension that makes them unable to confront it later on.

Despite his sense of humor, my father couldn't stand even the mere mention of death. If, over the course of a discussion, my mother ever referred to her own death, he would interrupt with a scathing "Stop talking nonsense!" As if a shrill sound had pierced his eardrum. "In many Jewish families, when someone falls ill, they're given another name. They change identities to deceive the supernatural being that might get the bad idea of coming to get them. The idea being that if the angel of death knocks at your door to ask for a certain Moshe, you can calmly reply, 'Sorry, there's no Moshe living here. This is Solomon's home.' Then the angel will apologize for bothering you and be on his way," relates the Rabbi Delphine Horvilleur in *Living with Our Dead*.
If my father had known this legend, for the last year of his life, he would have insisted we call him Freddie, Stan, or Lee. The names of his favorite jazz musicians. He'd been raised in a family of believers but was completely unfamiliar with the sacred texts. He was deeply atheistic. My brothers and I bear the holiest family name in Jewish culture without knowing a thing about the religion. Our father never spoke about it. And, faithful to family tradition, we never asked questions. Our connection with Judaism was the couscous my grandmother made once a year on Yom Kippur. We gobbled down the semolina and artichoke balls without the

slightest idea what the Day of Atonement meant.
The other holidays—Shabbat, Rosh Hashanah, or Hanukkah—weren't on our family calendar. A few years ago, a friend invited me to celebrate Passover with his family. The whole night, I introduced myself with only my first name—as goy as it gets—so as not to draw attention to my last name. As a Sephardi at an Ashkenazi dinner, I was nauseated by the stuffed carp, minced liver, and sheep head. I understood nothing about the holiday traditions. I felt like a bad Jew.
Why didn't my father pass on anything of his roots? He wasn't a believer, but Jewish tradition isn't necessarily linked to religion. You can be Jewish without being religious. I would have loved for him to tell us about the Exodus from Egypt, the exile of his people and our ancestors from Southern Europe to North Africa, for him to tell us about life in Tunisia, show us photos or the little home movies his uncle made. He could also have introduced us to other members of his family, and they would have filled us in. But my father had cut all ties with the people who reminded him of a past that was too painful. Driven out of his country at the age of 18, he knew he would never look back. He turned the page on his childhood and youth once and for all. To assimilate better. Of course, he got nostalgic at times. But he didn't talk about it. Whenever I asked questions, his answers were elusive. I could tell it was painful, so I didn't insist.

It took a long time before he agreed to return to his homeland and bring us to the traces of his past. We had to insist. He finally gave in.
From the moment we arrived at the airport, my father was made to feel unwelcome. His name, the most Jewish of us all, branded him. He almost turned back around. We encouraged him to focus on the essentials: showing us the places he grew up. The whitewashed building where his parents lived their whole life, his high school, the holiday family home beside the sea, the sweet shop that sold strawberry ice cream, the tuna sandwich shop, the doughnut seller. He was moved. But we could tell

something was broken.
To end our trip, we traveled south, to Djerba. Gustave Flaubert wrote, "In Djerba, the air is so mild it staves off death." We stayed in a hotel along the coast. One afternoon while playing soccer on the sand, my youngest brother ran back to our bungalow. The glass patio door was closed. He didn't notice and smashed straight through it. He crumpled to the floor, his face bloody. A deep gash ran from his left eye to the back of his skull. His head was sliced in two. A young doctor at the hotel offered to treat him and rushed him to his office. We waited in the next room. Forever. My parents, overwhelmed with worry, burst in. When they saw my brother's deformed face, they knew: the young doctor had stitched up the skin without suturing the severed vein. The bruising was spectacular. We leapt into a cab, heading to the closest city, where a brand-new hospital had opened two weeks before. Believe in miracles. My half-conscious brother rested his head on my mother's lap. She stroked his hair and kept talking to him so he wouldn't fall asleep. The journey lasted an eternity in the stifling heat. I kept glancing at my father in the passenger seat. Overwhelmed with anxiety, he urged the driver to go faster. He kept closing his eyes, was struggling to breathe. When we reached the hospital, my brother was whisked away into the emergency room. His operation lasted three hours. The surgeon finally joined us in the waiting room.
"Your son made it," he announced. My mother burst into tears.
"It was a close call," the surgeon added.

My father took this as a sign. Returning to his country had been a mistake. He decided never to set foot there again.
After the trip, he stopped talking about his past once more. Yet as death approached, I wonder if reconnecting with his roots might have helped calm his fear. His brother, with whom he shared a pathological anxiety, made this choice. When his brother's wife fell ill, he asked a rabbi friend if he could pray with him. The rabbi offered to bring him along to the synagogue to pray and bless the worshippers. My uncle told him he was

an atheist. How could he take the place of the rabbi when he didn't know the scriptures or even a word of Hebrew? The rabbi explained that, through his surname, my uncle belonged to the first tribe of Israel, which gave him the right to bless any Jew. Even the most pious. He taught my uncle how to phonetically pronounce the prayer and brought him to the synagogue. My uncle recited the blessing, and from that day forward, returned each Saturday, on Shabbat. He would generally arrive at the start of the ceremony, stay ten minutes, long enough to bless the congregation, and head off to do his weekend errands, leaving the "real" believers to their worship. Despite his prayers, my aunt succumbed to her illness rather quickly. But my uncle continued the weekly ritual until the end of his life.

My father, however, even at death's door never felt the need to reconnect with religion.

In my mother's family, the relationship with death was simpler. As he grew old, my maternal grandfather spoke openly about it. He was tired. He'd lost his wife early. Then four of his daughters, one after the other. He celebrated his eightieth birthday with little enthusiasm. His ninetieth, with lassitude. He'd done his time. He no longer felt adapted to the world. He said he'd be happy to go, that death was a part of life. He died at the age of ninety-four. The day before, he boarded a plane from Marseille, where he lived, to Paris to attend his grandson's wedding. After the ceremony, he went to my parents' house to stay. My mother had bought him the latest Prix Goncourt. He spent the evening reading by the fire, sipping a glass of Cointreau. The following day, my mother and he took a long walk. The Luxembourg Gardens, the fountains, the beehives. Then they went for lunch in the Latin Quarter. They sat down at a table for two in the back of the restaurant. At one table over was a large family with an elderly man my grandfather's age. They acknowledged each other with a polite nod of the head. After a green salad with walnuts, the waitress brought a steak and fries. My grandfather stabbed a potato with his fork, dipped it in the sauce, and popped it into his mouth to enjoy. He swallowed and began choking, as quietly as he could. My mother urged him to spit it out. He refused: he had his dignity. His heart stopped. He crumpled in his chair before my mother's eyes. When she tells the story today, she says, "He had a little heart problem. I have the same one. I'm so happy: it's the ideal way to go!"

My mother passed on to me her light attitude toward death. I am not worried. At 50-something, I feel like I've lived a full life. If everything were to stop tomorrow, I think I'd go peacefully. The psychotherapist Irvin Yalom has developed the idea that anxiety about death is proportional to our regrets. I have few regrets. I like the Epicurean idea that, "As long as we are here, death is not here, and when death comes, we have gone."

*

When my father returns to Paris at the end of August, the family doctor orders a new round of tests. I take him to the medical imaging center in the center of town. Once the series of scans is finished, the lab director invites us into his office to discuss the results.

"Send it to my house," my father replies as he slips out the door.

He never learns the results of these tests. He doesn't want to know. And mainly, he doesn't want anyone explaining that, over the summer, his cancer spread dramatically and is now in his liver, that treatment is no longer an option, and he will soon be dead. He sticks to the principle that denying reality will preserve the illusion of his eternal life.

For the first time since he began treatment, I sense his fear. His silence, his incapacity to verbalize his illness, his refusal to hear the doctors' verdict, all these things show the extent of his terror. The depths of his anxiety. An irrational fear he cannot fight, which grows with each passing day. Despite his weight loss, shortness of breath, and difficulty moving

around, he does not mention his state. He outright refuses to talk about it. He changes the topic the second we bring it up.
We decide to respect his wishes. As long as the news is bad, we keep our mouths shut. As long as he doesn't ask, we won't tell.

*

My father spends his days doing crosswords in an armchair he finds increasingly hard to get out of. He winces with every effort, no longer leaves the house, eats less and less. He continues to lose weight. His clothes hang loose. My mother offers to update his wardrobe. His clothing style has always been basic: beige dockers, blue shirt, and loafers. The same getup for fifty years.
My mother heads to a Japanese store for the basics. She buys three pairs of pants, three shirts, three pairs of underwear, and a sweater. When she returns, my father plays along and models his new outfits for her. She texts me a few snapshots of my father standing in the middle of the living room in his brand-new clothes. He looks lost.

As time passes, as his illness progresses, the weaker he gets and the less he talks.
From the start, he put himself in the doctors' hands. "I'm entrusting you with the job of treating me. You take care of me. You handle it. I understand it's serious. That's all I need to know."

Yet my father is not the type of person to avoid obstacles. He is brave. He likes a challenge, likes to negotiate, move mountains, change the course of events. Faced with death, however, he gives up. It's far too irrational an opponent. He refuses to fight and puts himself in the hands of fate. He's a man full of good sense, yet superstitious. A character trait he inherited from his mother. When we ate at my grandparents' home, it was out of the question to have 13 people at the table. If there turned out to be 13 of us, my grandmother would invite a surprise guest. And if she couldn't find one, she'd eat alone in the kitchen. She was also careful never to prick her finger on a needle, break a mirror, or chew gum at night for fear of the evil eye. She never stepped on manhole covers either. As for my father, he hated reading bad news. When he'd discover a plane crash in the papers, even if it happened halfway across the world, he couldn't stand anyone talking about it. He refused to fly for years. An uncontrollable fear that forced him to travel by car—statistically 1,300 times more dangerous than planes—by train or boat, regardless of the distance. The first time we planned to visit the United States as a family, he booked passage on the *Queen Elizabeth 2* for a six-day cruise. But shortly before our departure, the United Kingdom went to war with Argentina over the Falkland Islands. The ship was requisitioned to transport British troops. We had to wait 20 more years to cross the Atlantic. My father finally agreed to take a plane. Each trip, he methodically got drunk before takeoff and continued drinking onboard. I remember one time when, loaded on *boukha*—a Tunisian fig brandy—he plummeted from a walkway and nearly fractured his tailbone.

*

For his final journey, he lets himself be guided. His only demands concern the details of daily life and requests for food. He has no particular wishes concerning how his illness is treated. He is convinced that the doctors, his wife, and children will make the right decisions.

He functioned by omission. He never broached any important topics. Never confided any of his feelings. He shared nothing and expected nothing in return. My father focused on the present and continued believing in luck. In that last card in poker that, when dealt, would give you a win against all odds. When he was younger, he spent his weekends at the racetrack. He loved betting. Loved the adrenaline high he got from taking risks. Today, he latches on to this hope. As tiny as it is.

*

Against all expectations, he books tickets for Christmas vacation. A trip south with the entire family. Nonchangeable, nonrefundable tickets. "I can't wait until December," he asserts.

*

My mother, brothers, and I tackle the homestretch like a mission: our job is to do everything we can to keep him from suffering, physically as well as mentally.
For this purpose, we have to lie to him. And although we believe we're doing this for his own good and with his tacit consent, it's extremely frustrating. To save our father from his anxiety, we hold back at the time we most need to be close to him. The lack of exchange and impossibility of expressing our feelings—at the risk of arousing his suspicion—creates a barrier between us.

I remember one of my aunts, who died at home. My parents had set her up in the room abutting mine. In the two days before she died, I could hear her talking nonstop to my mother. They spoke in low voices. Unclear. I couldn't understand what they were saying. But I imagined my aunt asking my mother to look after her daughters. Explaining what she wanted for her funeral. Handling the organization of life without her. Thanking my mother for taking care of her. Reiterating her love. My mother thanked her, too. Thank you, my dear little sister, for being in my life. I love you, too.

All the things that never got said with my father.

THE FINAL STRETCH

The oncologist announces that my father isn't strong enough for another round of chemo. She recommends we transfer him to a palliative care unit. Out of the question. My mother won't hear of it. She made a promise. She swore he wouldn't go back to the hospital. He will not go back.

The very next day, she organizes in-home medical care: a nurse will come to provide daily care and our family doctor will make regular house calls.

We rearrange their room, hiding the medical paraphernalia as best as possible. My father can't stand anything that reminds him of illness. His meds go in a shoebox. The prescriptions, in the nightstand. The drip, under a sarong and out of his sight.

My mother, brothers, and I take turns at his side. We make sure he's never alone, never in need of anything. We bring him news from outside. Friends, the ones he no longer sees, family, the latest gossip. We make jokes, try to summon a bit of cheerfulness. Like before.

We provide what he seems to expect from us: a reassuring environment.

To coax our father out of his room, we cobble together a projection system in the living room. He's delighted. Makes him feel like he's out on the town. We choose lighthearted films, Italian comedies, his favorite. We rewatch *The Scientific Cardplayer* by Luigi Comencini.

But soon, he can no longer get out of bed. He is too weak to walk. It's harder and harder for him to wash on his own. He can't stand seeing himself in the mirror anymore. He no longer gets on the scale, after a lifetime of being obsessed with his weight.

"They're not treating me!" he protests to my mother. Since the start of this whole business, he's never complained. He's always been grateful to the doctors, thanking them regularly. But now he's angry. "When am I going to start chemo again?"

It's the first time he's shown disgust. The first time he puts words to his illness. Is he finally going to open up? Ask for explanations? Has the time come to tell him the truth? Explain that the evolution of his illness has little to do with how the doctors are treating him? That he's in the best possible hands? Everyone's trying their hardest? We could use the opportunity to suggest alternative treatments. Instinct therapy, magnetic therapy, naturopathy, a Brazilian shaman. One of my aunts went on a three-month Ayurvedic cure in the mountains; it would be easy to find out the name of the place. We could also ask our father about what comes next. Organize the end of his life together. But where do we start? Announcing the terrible results of his last tests? The doctors' disastrous conclusions? Admit that, despite everyone's best intentions, there's nothing anyone can do for him? We don't have the guts. Hearing that would do him in. So we remain elusive.

"You need to build up your strength so the oncologist can develop a new plan of action," we lie.

In hindsight, I wonder what would have happened if we'd come clean at that moment.

No doubt it would have been a relief. The weight of silence grew heavier by the day. But my father could not face such a revelation. It would have crushed him. His denial was like a shield that kept him from sinking into terror and depression, as his own father did. And I tell myself that, despite the frustration and sadness it engendered for me, I'm happy to have respected the folly he'd established. It was in keeping with who he was. His way of facing death.

*

During his initial weeks of bed rest, my father agreed to have visitors. People hurried to his bedside. Some spoke of the future, others of the past, and still others continued to seek his advice. A niece asked him about renovations to her new studio, and he made a sketch in her datebook. An aunt showed him her latest financial statement, and he got out the calculator. A friend described his new project for a restaurant, my father promised to visit as soon as possible. A cousin brought him Tunisian pastries without realizing he could no longer eat sugar. Everyone tried their hardest to embrace life, pretending not to notice his increasingly sunken cheeks and yellowing skin.

All the coming and going finally gets to him. The parade of people past his bedside alarms him. Like a bad omen. By keeping them away, he keeps death at bay. And he doesn't want anyone seeing him in this condition anymore. People can visit again once he's doing better.

From now on, only his wife, sister, and sons are allowed to enter his room.

*

My father sleeps all day and lies awake most of the night.

*

My aunt insists on visiting. My father agrees to make an exception.
She arrives in the early afternoon, sits beside his bed, and suggests they look at photos from the past.
He gets into it.
For hours, they flip through old photo albums. My father asks my mother to bring the black-and-white pictures of his childhood in Tunisia and his arrival in Paris in his late teens, the Kodachrome snapshots yellowing with time, me as a baby with chubby cheeks —my mother had insisted I eat one egg per day—the birth of my brothers, our summers in my grandfather's house in Provence, winter sports, our weddings, the arrival of grandchildren.

Reminiscing about the people he loves, those who now can only be seen in photos, puts a smile back on his face. He recalls old trips, forgotten beaches, and distant celebrations, in search of lost emotions. He could see this procession of his life as something premonitory and morbid. Bringing up all these happy moments might make his approaching death even more cruel. On the contrary, the succession of memories soothes him. Turning toward the past to avoid thinking of the future.

*

Time flows between soccer and the images of sixty-nine years of life. My father has more and more trouble sitting up on his own. He can no longer turn over in bed and must sleep on his back. He snores.

*

On nights when he can't sleep, he watches television. For hours. With the sound off. So as not to wake my mother. He watches one muted sports program after another.

*

My mother tries to give him massages. But he won't let her. He can't bear to have anyone touch him. Like a wounded animal.

*

New aches and pains emerge. The doctor gives him morphine tablets. My father fears the return of the ominous figures. We reassure him. We're here; we'll protect him.

*

My father dozes most of the time, barely talks anymore.

*

One evening, after a particularly trying day, I meet my wife and some friends for a night out. I let off steam, drink, a lot, dance, a little. I party while my father is dying.

*

The present stretches into the simultaneously dilated and accelerated rhythm of the end of a life. Too long. Too short. We know that what is happening will happen too soon. It's always too soon. Before the summer, the surgeon spoke of a few months. Now we count in days. We try to make the most of these final moments, but we're sentenced to silence. We helplessly watch his decline.
The unbearable situation drags on.

*

A week later, my father is still here.

*

He grows weaker by the day. Then suddenly, a burst of energy. He asks to get out of bed. He wants to go downstairs to watch a movie. We carry him to the living-room couch.
I try to find a story that can gently accompany his revival, that makes no reference to death or illness, without any hospitals, funerals, or plane crashes. No easy task. I settle on *Tamara Drewe*. A British comedy. Spirited and light. My father laughs a lot. For a couple of hours, he forgets everything.

When it's over, he wants to eat dinner at the table with us. He presides. Radiant. He doesn't eat much. Doesn't talk much. He looks at us, listens, smiles. He feels alive once more.
He dozes off before dessert.
We take him back up to his room.

*

From that day on, he never leaves his bed.

*

To pass the time, my youngest brother offers to organize the mess of papers on his desk. A way for him to delve into the accounts he'll soon be in charge of. My father is relieved to get in order the documents he hasn't touched for months. He is usually incredibly organized and meticulous. My brother discovers entire binders full of bank statements, some over 20-years old. He suggests getting rid of the oldest ones.
"When do you think these old papers are going to be useful?"
My father is annoyed and snaps at him. My brother lets it go; he knows it's nothing personal, that my father can't stand to be in a position of dependence. My brother sucks it up. He wants to make the most of these final moments alone with his father. Throughout his childhood, my brother strove to find a connection with him. But our father was annoyed by a son he struggled to understand. It took years for him to earn our father's respect and finally his admiration. Today, now that they've finally forged a strong bond, he's going to disappear.
For several hours, they index and file contracts, deeds, company statutes, bank letters, until my father gets worn out and dozes off once more.
When it's time to go home, my brother, alone in the street, bursts into tears. He's had it. He can't take talking to his father about nothing but financial accounts and letters of credit.

*

One Sunday, a few days before his death, my other brother and I spend the afternoon with our father watching television. Manchester United beats Liverpool three to two in the final minutes. Hat trick by the Bulgarian Dimitar Berbatov. Chelsea kills Blackpool. Four to zero. Next we turn to the Italian championship to watch Lazio's victory over Fiorentina. My brother leaves at halftime during this last game, having ODed on soccer. As he leaves the room, my father calls out:

"Thank you, son."

My brother turns and replies.

"No, it's me who should thank you, Dad."

Their way of saying goodbye.

We each expressed our farewell in our own way, carefully avoiding any direct reference to it. One of us through encouraging words between bank statements. The other with a simple "thank you." And me, by being at his side when he breathed his last.

My mother didn't like the idea of last goodbyes. When I questioned her ten years later, she said, "For 50 years, we never stopped talking. We didn't need to say anything more."

*

I sit on the edge of the bed. Alone with my father. He has cramps in his legs. I hand him a painkiller and glass of water.

"I'm sorry," he says. "For what?"

He shrugs.

This is the moment to talk.

I could say, "How do you feel?"

He would reply, "Son, I'm dying. I know it's over. There's nothing anyone can do. But I want you to help me go gently. To stay by my side. Until the very end. I'm sorry I didn't say all that earlier. I couldn't. It's too hard. Too stupid, mainly. We had wonderful things yet to do together. . . . Take care of your mother. She's going to need you. . . . You have to return to Italy. Say goodbye to everyone for me. Eat one last lemon ice for me. Promise?" And he would end with, "I love you."

Impossible to say the least little word.

I would feel like I was breaking a pact. Betraying everyone. My father, mother, brothers. And even if I had the guts to ask him, he probably would have dodged the issue. Replied "so-so" in a banal tone of voice.

Why such stubbornness? What is he afraid of? Not being up to it? Influencing fate? Having a panic attack? Howling in terror like his father? What's going on in this man's mind? Is it possible he has hope?

The only thing that's sure: he is not ready. Not to talk, nor to die.

My father's brother, a decade later, will be even more radical. He'll hide his cancer from his loved ones until a few weeks before his death. Yet, as a doctor, he should have known that acknowledging illness significantly increases your chances of recovery. To conquer an enemy, you must identify it as such.

I feel my father's hand rest on mine. A simple, rare gesture that means he's tired.

He gives me a faint smile and dozes off.

I observe him. He looks like a little boy. His features are soft, his skin, smooth. Despite his fatigue, he faithfully shaves each morning, dragging the electric razor over his hollow cheeks for a few long minutes. Even if no one visits anymore, he wouldn't dream of letting himself go. That would be giving in.

His breathing is regular. The corner of his mouth twitches into a smile. What thought has just gone through his mind? What is he dreaming about? Places he can no longer go?

The dance floor of a New York salsa club? A soccer stadium on game night? The terrace of a restaurant along the ocean? A hill in Tuscany?

The warm water of the Mediterranean?
A beach? Any beach. He loved them all.
My mother's body? How long has it been since they last made love?
Or death?

I fall asleep beside him. My turn to dream.
Of a house in the south. My grandfather's.
The heat is stifling. The cicadas are loud.
My bare feet on a gravel patio.
A path leads to a cherry orchard.
A pile of stones at the start of a path. Massive rocks piled into a pyramid.
A mound several feet high. Beneath the rocks: a fire. A giant furnace.
Dark shapes move in the flames. Bodies.
An inferno of human flesh. No odor.
Just a vibration. Unbearable.
A deafening sound that pierces my skull.
The recurrent nightmare of my childhood. The one I'd have whenever my fever climbed very high. Each time, the charred corpses reappeared.
It's been ages since those images haunted me.
I wake up with a heavy head.
My father hasn't moved. He's still breathing.

THE DECISION

"It's the end."

The doctor is explicit.

"We've exhausted all therapeutic treatments. His body will decline quickly in the coming days. He'll experience more and more pain. The final 24 hours will likely be very difficult. For him, obviously. But for you as well."

"How long?"

"A week. Tops."

My mother is furious.

"I know he's going to die, but not so fast, it can't be." She gets worked up. She compares the experience with that of her youngest sister, whose life she managed to prolong with last-minute intervention. There simply must be a way. I think of my New York friend, of François Mitterrand, all the people given up for dead who lived several years more.

"Unfortunately, there is no question," the doctor insists.

Of course. My mother knows. She has watched her husband degrade day after day, like all of us. She couldn't help being hopeful.

Now, it's over.

"When is the real suffering going to start?" she asks. "Soon."

*

When the nurse comes to administer my father's daily care, my mother, brothers, and I seize the opportunity to go out for lunch. As soon as we leave the house, my youngest brother bursts into tears once more. My other brother puts an arm around his shoulders. I take my mother's arm.

We walk down the street, shell-shocked. We sit on the terrace of the nearest café and order drinks. We are mute for a long time. We exchange lost looks. There are no words to express our pain. So we say nothing. My mother takes a few sips of her beer and decides to break the silence.

"I will not let him suffer."

We agree. We must take action, before it's too late. We don't know how yet, but there has to be a way. This is the 21st century. Science has progressed since my aunts died. Nowadays, there must be some way of letting the terminally ill go in peace. Our ignorance makes us confident. We have no idea that thousands of people still die in terrible condition in this country. That despite new laws providing for sedation, 26 French departments are not equipped for palliative care. That only one-fifth of the people who request hospice have access to it. That the administrative complexity and lack of funds mean that most French people receive no actual care. That, even though doctors are supposed to treat the terminally ill, many stick to protocol, refusing to go any further. That the only way to die peacefully at home is to fall back on what is called "illegal euthanasia." That most people die in great distress in ill-equipped institutions. For centuries, people died at home; it wasn't a problem for anyone. Today, those who make this choice are ostracized. They must figure it out on their own. Like in the days of back-alley abortions.

We are also unaware that the practice of cutting someone's life short, even with the best of intentions, even by a matter of hours, is considered murder.

We innocently think that what we are about to do simply stands to reason: letting a loved one go without suffering.

"However, not a word to your father," my mother adds. "He absolutely cannot know. It would kill him."

Of course, I think. Let's spare him.

"Don't you think it's kind of complicated to prematurely end Dad's life without telling him?" objects my youngest brother.

My mother turns to him in surprise. Given our father's attitude from the start of his illness, his refusal to address the subject, and his fear of facing facts, the decision seems obvious. Clearly this isn't the case.

"Your father discussed it with me," my mother finally says.

We stare at her openmouthed.

She tells us, many years ago, after watching one of my aunts agonized in her deathbed and finally suffocating to death, how my father opened up to her.

"He told me, 'I never want to go through that. If I ever wind up in that situation, I'm counting on you to do what needs to be done. But I never want to discuss it again.'"

II

THE REQUEST

On the morning of Friday, September 15, my mother calls our doctor.

"We need you. We want you to help him go peacefully before he suffers too much."

"I can't do that."

"I watched my sisters suffer for nothing. I won't let it happen again. Please help us."

The doctor pauses.

"Even if I agreed, I don't have the supplies I need."

"What do you need?"

"Midazolam. It's used for general anesthesia. I have a little at the office, but not enough for what you're asking. The problem is you can only get it at the hospital, which isn't . . ."

I interrupt.

"I'm on it."

*

I call my father-in-law, an anesthesiologist and head of the emergency department at a Parisian hospital.

"That's a complicated request."

"There's no one else we can ask."

"Are you sure of what you're doing?"

"Positive."

He thinks about it.

"All right. I'll help you. However, I can't give it to you at the hospital. It's too risky."

We plan to meet the next morning on the square outside Notre-Dame.

*

It took me several years to question the seriousness of this decision. Can you help someone die who isn't ready to die? Can you, under the pretext of protecting them from their own anxiety, make such a decision in their stead? Though I know some people are against the idea, that they believe we shouldn't interfere with nature, God's will, or simply that we must obey the law, I am convinced even today that we made the right choice. Of course, we would rather have discussed it with him, decided together, known his last wishes. But we felt it wasn't possible. My mother had spent 50 years with him. She understood his silences, his looks, his movements. She knew what suited our father better than anyone. He confided in her.

*

Later that day, I run into my father's sister in the hallway with a CD in her hand.

"Your father heard this song by Barbara on the radio yesterday. He seemed moved. I went out and bought him the album this morning."

Today, every time my aunt hears that song, she cries.

When those we love
Now close their eyes
And the time has come, Oh, grant at least
Their final prayer May they go to sleep
In peace, in peace.

My father must have known. There's no way he didn't understand what the words meant. His emotions came from these explicit lyrics. Were we all putting on an act that this man, who had set the rules of the game, no longer believed in? Death was staring him in the face yet he carried on as if it didn't concern him. "Sorry, there's no Moshe living here. This is Solomon's home."

My aunt asks me to give him the CD for her. She thinks she's coming down with something. She doesn't want to put him at risk. She'll come back in a few days when she's feeling better. I take her to the kitchen and explain the situation.

She collapses into a chair. Tears stream down her cheeks. She catches her breath and admits her shock—she hadn't understood the full extent of the situation. When she visited my parents in central France that summer, she thought her brother seemed weak, but she figured the treatment in the fall would get him back on his feet. The old family habit of refusing to look truth in the eye.

It's unthinkable. Since she was a little girl, she'd always imagined her brother would live to be 90. Maybe even a 100. When he was diagnosed, she thought perhaps his life would be a bit shorter than she had imagined. But nothing like this.

She thanks me for telling her the truth and laments her brother's refusal to talk.

"That's the problem with silent families," she adds.

I tell her our intention to not let our father suffer. We're going to help him go. She stares at me wide-eyed and starts to cry again.

A few years later, she'll tell me she didn't agree with the decision.

"For me, as long as there's a breath of life, there is life. As long as the person is still here, we don't know what's going on in their soul. As long as they're here, they exist."

She also spoke about her mother's death.

My grandmother, afflicted with cerebral degeneration spent the last weeks of her life at my aunt's house. My aunt slept next to her every night. My father and uncle didn't come visit: they were in denial. When my aunt sensed the end was near, she asked her brothers to come see their mother one last time. My uncle refused. "There's no point," he said. "She won't remember." My father finally made the trip. In horror, he discovered his mother's skeletal form and emaciated face. He turned around almost immediately. As he left, he told his sister, "Don't ever do that to me again, you understand?" A few days before she died, while she was in a semicoma, my grandmother took her daughter's hand and whispered, "You're not pregnant." My aunt, who was having trouble conceiving, had recently had IVF without telling anyone.

"You see, even when you think it's over, things can happen. . . . I don't blame you, but I feel like you deprived me of two or three days more with my brother."

*

My mother and I go out for dinner alone while my brothers stay home with our father.

We make a list of priorities:

- Get the drug.
- Decide with the doctor when the "procedure" will take place.
- Summon the family.

We feel our way along, forced to improvise. The situation is unbearable. Why should we have to go through this? Why does our society allow us to choose how we live but not how we die? Why does it protect us throughout our life, forcing us to wear a helmet on a motorcycle, a seat belt in a car, get vaccinated against serious diseases, if only to abandon us at the moment of death?

We're bewildered, yet we never question our decision. Are we afraid of changing our minds? Afraid of losing our nerve? Or is it simply that self-evident? What's the alternative? Life whatever the cost? For what? For whom? For him? So he can waste away in bed with nothing but decline on the horizon? For us? To enjoy a few more hours or days with him? Enjoy? Or endure? Permanently ruin the last image we'll have of him? Bring him back to the hospital? So his death can be enveloped in some sort of haze? Terminal sedation, they call it. At home, it's murder. At the hospital, it's relief of suffering. My mother was clear: he stays home. "I don't want an intern to make this decision for me."

It's mild out. We sit on the patio. My mother isn't hungry. I make up for it. I have a habit of eating and drinking when stressed. Tonight, country pâté, chateaubriand with peppercorn sauce, fries, and a bottle of Burgundy red. My mother doesn't touch her food.

"Maybe it's the right time." It slips out.

"The right time for what?" she asks.

"The right time for him. To go. Dad always hated getting old, he couldn't stand losing his hair, losing at tennis, becoming physically diminished. He's getting more and more bitter, even harsh at times. With you. With the kids, too. He's impatient and can't tolerate the least aggravation."

My mother stares at me, lost. "Maybe," she whispers.

The past few years were painful for my father. After they sold their children's clothing brand, he sank into depression. The man who didn't believe in psychotherapy or psychoanalysis—who would say, whenever we'd talk about someone who was depressed, "He needs to make an effort"—broke down. He continued to resist the idea of seeing a specialist but agreed to take some pills. In spite of this, he never completely recovered his *joie de vivre.*

My mother pours herself a glass of wine.

"A few weeks ago, we had a horrible argument," she says. "We were driving along the river, he got out and walked off. All the cars were honking. I panicked. I didn't know what to do. I figured he'd come back but he didn't. He disappeared. I'd like to be a saint, accept being mistreated, but I can't."

Before the summer, we'd spent a weekend in the country. Family only. My father had been extremely tough on my mother. When we got back to Paris, I wrote him a letter.

Dad,
I never thought one day I would have to send you this kind of letter but the weekend we just spent together was so hard that I needed to write.
I understand you're exhausted by your illness, that your fatigue grates on your nerves. And having seven kids in the house for a whole weekend doesn't help. The fact that you're impatient and snap at them doesn't shock me. They're not babies. They know you love them. On the other hand, I think your behavior with Mom is extremely unfair. For months she's been taking care of you without asking for anything in return. She looks after you. She caters to your every whim. And with the smallest problem, you treat her like a dog. And I'm weighing my words.
I know you love her deeply, that you're grateful she's by your side fighting this horrible disease, so I beg you, don't be unfair. It's too brutal. For her obviously, but for us, too. It's unbearable to see you treat her like that. It's not like you.
The next time you're angry or lose your patience, please think of this letter and spare her. She still needs a lot of strength and love to support you in this battle that you're going to win together.
We're here, too. I love you.
B.

He simply replied, "I'm sorry."

It's dusk. I end my meal with crepes suzette flambéed with Grand Marnier.
"He's had a wonderful life," my mother concludes.
It's true. My father has lived fully. He can go peacefully, with no regrets.

A few days later, I bring up to my youngest brother that maybe our father dying now is not such bad timing, that this way he won't "age poorly." He reacts vehemently.
"What kind of bullshit is that? Dad should have another ten years, maybe even 20."

He means: Dad should never die.

Today when we talk about it, he says, "I agreed with the decision. But you and Mom took charge of it. As the oldest son, you stepped up."

My other brother has few memories of this period. He tried to block out the episode from his mind. That's how he operates. He forgets anything that encroaches on his happiness. In the morning, when he wakes up, he thinks about what makes him happy. We inherited this culture of pleasure. My father called it fun. Fun was the pillar of our lives. What my brother mainly remembers is that he did not oppose the idea of helping our father go, yet did nothing to contribute either. "I had the feeling we were out of line and I rather liked that," he said. I remind him, paraphrasing Jean-Luc Godard, that it's the margin that holds the pages together. It makes him smile. At the time, I had no idea that a few years later, the famous New Wave filmmaker would die by assisted suicide at his home in Switzerland at the age of 91. He wasn't even ill, merely tired, and he chose to die of his own free will.

As for me, I didn't hesitate. I'd watched my aunts die, friends of my parents, too, heard countless stories about painful ends, and I had the deep-seated conviction that we were doing what was best for our father. I'm proud of what we accomplished, even if proud is probably not quite the right word. Recently, I read an essay Dr. Léon Schwartzenberg wrote, relating how he helped several of his patients die. Someone asked him, "Are you proud of yourself?" to which he replied, "No, I'm not proud, but if I hadn't done it, I'd be ashamed of myself." I think that today, a lot of people, mainly politicians, should share this shame.

Since then, I've thought about my own death. I don't want to suffer either. No one wants to suffer. I've talked to my loved ones about it: I absolutely do not want any intensive-care medication. I joined an association for the right to die with dignity and have researched the options of legal—and illegal—euthanasia and the medical cocktails available. I'm ready. Or at least, I thought I was. But a recent discussion with my father-in-law rocked my convictions. As a long-term sufferer of Parkinson's, for years he asserted that as soon as he could no longer walk or see, he'd take measures. For him, as an anesthesiologist, it would be a mere formality. But today, in a wheelchair and practically blind, he's changed his mind. "I'll stick it out until the end," he says. The fact that this man—who, throughout his career, rubbed shoulders with death and witnessed such suffering—would be so attached to life, disturbed me. What if, when the time comes, I also have this change of heart? It's hard for me to believe it today. But I am less adamant. How can we know what goes on in the mind of someone who feels their life is ending until we experience it ourselves?

*

I meet my father-in-law outside the cathedral. He discreetly slips a small vial into the pocket of my jacket.

"Whatever you do, don't tell anyone. It's a huge risk. I could be banned from the Council of the Order of Physicians for something like this."

I nod.

"A few weeks ago," he adds, "when I stopped by to see your father, he told me he wanted to go before it got too painful. He was terrified by the thought of suffering." I don't believe him. My father-in-law is trying to alleviate my guilt, and I'm grateful for it. But my father would never have spoken so openly about death, especially his own. He did it once, reluctantly, with my mother and never mentioned it again. He was walled up in his silence, but expressed his feelings in other ways. One afternoon, my wife found herself sitting on his bed watching a tennis match—there was no soccer that day—and my father held her hand a long time. He squeezed it tight, without a word. She felt if she hadn't removed it, he would have held it forever. It was his way of telling her he loved her. To my knowledge, he was never more expressive than that.

Before we part, my father-in-law whispers in my ear, “It’s good what you’re doing.”

I walk back to my parents’ apartment. The time it takes to get there is interminable. I trudge along like a zombie, my hands in my pockets. In the left, my phone and keys. In the right, the drug that will soon kill my father.

TAKING ACTION

Coffee in the kitchen. The doctor sits between my mother and me. He has just examined my father. He confirms what we already know. His state is worsening, at high speed.

"When would you like me to step in?" he asks. My mother sighs.

The time it takes to gather close family. Brothers, sisters-in-law, our aunt, our uncle. We'll spare the children.

"Tomorrow. 9pm?"

*

It's the last night. She knows. He does not.

She observes him in his sleep. Studies his corpselike body. There's practically nothing left of his sweet face, his muscular arms, his manly physique, his keen gaze.

The more she looks, the more it breaks her heart. She wants to touch him. Hold him tight. She can't stand seeing him diminished anymore. Watching him waste away. Watching him die.

My father's eyes flutter open. He catches her looking.

"You okay?" he whispers.

"Yes, dear. Go back to sleep."

*

Last breakfast. A cup of tea. Fresh-squeezed lemon.

She knows. He does not.

*

Last lunch. A cup of vegetable broth. Stewed fruit.
We know. He does not.
My father struggles to get the fruit down. It is increasingly difficult for him to swallow. Each mouthful is an ordeal. He hasn't had the IV drip in for days. All he can eat are stewed apples and pears with a bit of lemon. It's the zest he likes best. He sucks on them for minutes before chewing them slowly.
He smiles at us.
Don't break down. Don't cry. Whatever we do. Not when we're this close.

*

The doctor arrives in the afternoon. "Are you ready?" he asks my mother. She is speechless. Incapable of answering such a question. She reminds me of a character in a Krzysztof Kieślowski film, *A Short Film about Killing.* A lawyer defends a murderer. The young criminal is sentenced to death. The lawyer visits him one last time in prison. The execution is scheduled for after their visit, which the lawyer drags out as long as he can even while the guards pressure him to hurry up. The warden finally comes to ask when they'll be finished talking. The lawyer replies, "Never." The guards burst into the cell and march the prisoner to the gallows.
The doctor explains that he is going to give my father a drip to administer the drug slowly. Morphine and Valium will gradually put him to sleep. Then he'll be induced into a coma. At that point, the doctor will add the midazolam, which will gently stop his heart. The whole process will take about six hours.
"What are you going to tell him?" my mother asks.
"A half-lie. It bothers me a little not to tell him the truth, but when a patient doesn't want to know, I respect their wishes."

Near 3pm, the doctor asks if we want to go up with him. My mother would rather not. I go along.

We enter the room. My father is dozing. I sit down on the side of his bed. The doctor tries to sit him up. He grasps him under the arms. My father wraps his skinny arms around the doctor's neck but is so weak that they immediately fall back. His muscles no longer respond. The doctor asks me to help. My father merely shrugs at this humiliating situation. I am shaken and go back to the other side of the bed. I pick up a magazine and nervously flip through it. I come upon photos commemorating the anniversary of 9/11. Nine years already. 2,977 people dead. An abstract number. Here, I am staring a reality in the face. One man is about to die. And that man is my father.

The doctor nods slightly, indicating the time has come.

He leans close to my father and straightens his head.

"How are you doing this afternoon?"

"So-so."

"I'm going to put the drip back in."

"Really? Why?"

Dad glances at me. I wink.

"To rehydrate you," the doctor reassures him. "We're going to get your strength back."

My father smiles. "Wonderful," he says.

Does he really think that what is happening is "wonderful"? Does he think this drip is going to get him back on his feet? That it will allow him to continue the chemo, to be cured, to live? I'll never know. On the other hand, he surely doesn't imagine that this is his last word. That a few seconds later, he'll fall asleep, never to wake up again.

At that moment, I have no idea how the next few hours are going to play out. I don't know how my father is going to die. But I sense that this last word is a benediction. He says, "My life has been wonderful." He thanks us. "What you're doing for me is wonderful." He encourages us. "I'm relying on you to make the rest as wonderful as what we've experienced

together." Or maybe he knows it's the end? And he's saying, "It's wonderful to finish like this."
As if this word had been the leitmotif of his existence. As if all the values he instilled in us, all the energy he passed on to us, all his joy of life, his optimism—despite his anxiety—his kindness, gentleness, and humor could all be summed up in a single word.
Wonderful: that is entirely him.

DEATH

Saturday night.
The family has gathered.
My mother and I.
My two brothers and their wives. My father's sister.
My uncle is not there. He chose not to be present.
My wife is absent, too. Stuck in traffic. She sobs in the back of a taxi and apologizes to the driver.
"I'm losing someone."
We wait, huddled on the couches around the coffee table in the living room, like in a movie. Seven spectators waiting for capital punishment, motionless behind a window.
No one speaks.
The silence is unusual. Even at the darkest moments, we always managed to crack a joke. Humor is a force of resistance in all circumstances. Tonight, however, we are incapable.

My brother opens a bottle of wine. The others barely touch it. I down one glass after another.

*

What's going on up there?
My mother went up ten minutes ago. The doctor was
sitting beside the bed, monitoring my father's evolving state. He was still breathing but no longer moving.

*

A half hour later, the doctor enters the room. He asks me to come. Why me? Why just me? Because I'm the oldest? The accomplice? The dealer? I get up and follow him. We climb the stairs to the second floor.

He pauses outside the door to talk to me. He says he's going to keep his promise. He will see it through, take the necessary steps, and then he will go. He cannot sign the death certificate. It's too dangerous. He suggests that, once it's over, we call another doctor to come certify my father's death.

"Do you know any GPs in the neighborhood?"

"Yes. We've been unfaithful at times."

He smiles.

"He's the one you should call."

We enter the room.

My father is lying in the semidarkness.

"Is he alive?"

"Yes," the doctor replies somberly.

I let out a sigh of relief.

"Not for much longer," he adds.

I look at my father's chest slowly rising and falling. I step close to him. His face is pale, serene. His features hollow, his mouth cracked open. The mouth that will no longer laugh. His breathing is regular. No sign of suffering.

How can I imagine that in a few minutes, he will no longer be "of this world?" Here yet already no longer here? I do my best to hold it together. But I can finally let down my guard. I no longer have to worry about worrying him. The tears don't come. I'll cry later. Much later. For now, I am cut off from my emotions. I wall up, won't let myself crack. I won't break down until my cat dies, two years after my father. I remember wandering around my apartment, sobbing inconsolably with no idea why.

"It's now," the doctor whispers.

My father's breathing is weak but regular. He inhales and exhales three times. Suddenly he takes a deeper breath followed by a long exhale. An audible rale. His last breath. I am filled with profound sadness and absolute relief.

I am shattered. Cannot tear my eyes from him. I cling to the moment. So many people regret the last memory they have of their loved ones. But I will never forget the serenity.

*

The father I loved so.

*

Death is an abstract thing. You learn someone has died. Yesterday they were alive. Today they are dead.
Before, life. After, death.
Before what? After what?
Now I know.
It's my first time.
I was deeply marked by the disappearance of other family members and close friends, but this is the first time that I've witnessed death directly, that I feel such a void, like suction in my chest. I've seen actors die on film. I've read accounts and stories that describe the split second when everything changes. I imagined something excruciating. It clearly must be grueling to watch someone die. Especially your father.
On the contrary. Right now, I feel a deep sense of peace.
The doctor knew. He knew the importance of this image. He knew it would forever remain engraved in my memory. That the serenity of the moment would ease the pain. That the journey we made together, the strength it took for us to come to this decision, to see our project through, required a powerful, soothing conclusion. A liberation. He gave me a gift.

*

Several minutes go by. I haven't moved. I am still at the side of the bed, next to my father's dead body. A thought crosses my mind: I must now learn to be an orphan. All my life, I've known my father alive. Already, I can no longer hear his voice. I realize that what terrifies me most in what's just transpired is not the loss of the future but the loss of the past. Our past. I've lost an entire swath of my history.

For a few minutes, he is present. A few hours maybe. But soon, he'll be gone. And little by little, as was the case for the others, his face, his voice, his laugh will be nothing but a vague memory.

*

It's my job to announce our father's death. I start down the stairs, the bearer of bad tidings. I pause halfway down. For a few seconds, my mother, brothers, wife, aunt, and sisters-in-law are in the limbo of the world before. A world in which my father lives.

As I descend the final steps, I spot my family through the living-room door that stands ajar. My mother senses my presence. She turns her head. I beckon her to come.

She's the first to enter the room. She pauses when she discovers the inert body of the love of her life, his mouth agape.

She ventures forward. Strokes his face. Tries to close his mouth, but his jaw falls back open.

"He would hate to be seen like this."

She disappears into the bathroom. Returns holding a scarf. She lifts his chin, wraps the scarf around his head, and ties a knot on top. An Easter egg. She wants him to look good in all circumstances.

Even dead.

Now that my father is "presentable," the others approach. My youngest brother sobs in his wife's arms. He is overwhelmed and hangs back. My other brother, silent, quickly strokes my father's hand and leaves the room. My turn. I don't move.

It's not him. Yet it is him, still.

I drink in his face one last time. Imprint it on my mind. As much as possible. I look at a body that contains a whole lifetime. This man soon to be reduced to ash. That, too, he didn't plan for. He never would have been able to deal with that sort of practical detail. Like the rest of it, we decided for him. My mother has planned to bury his urn in the garden of their country home. At the foot of a tree where a rosebush grows.

I go back down to the living room and join the rest of the family. The doctor hugs my mother and leaves. I catch up to him in the hallway.

"I want to thank you. You made the unbearable almost bearable."

He admits it's the only time he's helped someone die who did not clearly express their wishes. But he says that, given the chance, he would do it again. He knows exactly what stage my father was at. It seemed fair to spare him the suffering. Physically speaking as well as mentally. He respects the fact that my father didn't want to know. He says it's unfair to go in pain, in a state of physical deterioration. He recognizes that we shortened the end of my father's life. But by what? A week? At most. He was bedridden. He'd lost his autonomy. He hardly ate anymore. Could barely drink. As a doctor, he thinks that accompanying someone at the end of their life is like accompanying them during their life. Dying well is as important as living well. He tells me that euthanasia means "good death" in Greek.

"You can call the doctor now."

Meanwhile, he advises me to close the windows in the bedroom, turn the lights out, and the heat off.

"And take care of your mother," he adds before he steps out the door.

As I watch him go, I think of the months that have passed since my father's diagnosis. Exactly nine. Nine months to die. A gestation in reverse.

*

I find my mother alone in the kitchen. She asks me to tell her how Dad went.

"Extremely peacefully. Mission accomplished."

She hugs me.

"Most people finish their lives alone," she says. "They die in the hospital. Others go to Switzerland or Belgium. Imagine the nightmare. Taking the train on a one-way ticket to the beyond. They end up in a cold room surrounded by strangers. He was lucky not to go through that. He instead reached out to me, assuming we would have tea together the next morning. Then he fell asleep. How wonderful!"

AFTER

Ten years later, my mother, brothers, and I meet up in the Italian village where we took our summer vacations. It's the first time that we've returned since my father died. After he was gone, my mother declared she would never set foot there again. It took that long to convince her.

The night we arrive, we go for dinner along the river. We take the road that winds up the mountain and dips back down to the mouth of the Magra. I'm at the wheel, and my mother sits in the passenger seat, with my two brothers in back. The radio is going full blast. We belt out all our favorite Italian pop hits at the top of our lungs.

At sunset, we come out onto the little road that runs along the river. The beauty of the scenery, charged with so many memories, takes our breath away.

When we enter the restaurant, the owner greets us warmly. As if we'd been there just yesterday. Once we're seated at an outdoor table, halfway between the river and the sea, an old waiter brings a bottle of the white wine we used to drink way back when.

"*Dov'è il nonno?*" he asks. Where is grandpa?

"*Il nonno è morto,*" my brother replies.

Before the waiter can offer his condolences, we raise our glasses.

"*Alla salute del nonno!*"

The waiter pours himself a swallow of wine to toast with us.

We take a quick glance at the menu. There again, nothing has changed.

When it's time to order, my mother is overcome with a wave of emotion. In this place where everything has remained the same for a decade, the absence of our father is overwhelming.

"Thank you, kids," she says. "It's so great to be here with you. Your father gave me Italy."

As we start a second bottle, I take the plunge.

"I'd like to write a book about Dad. About how we helped him go."

My youngest brother sighs.

"Wow, that's intense. You sure it's a good idea?"

"I think it's good to share our story. I learned recently that what we did is considered a crime in the eyes of the law. I think it's important to tell the world that still, today, this act of absolute love is considered murder."

"I think it's a great idea," my mother pipes up. My other brother stays quiet.

"Since we're all together, the four of us, I thought it'd be a good time to talk about it."

"Or not," says the youngest. He turns to my mother.

"Mom, does it bother you to talk about this?"

"Not at all. On the contrary. It's good to talk about Dad tonight."

The waiter arrives pushing a metal cart with a salt-baked fish on it. He prepares the fish at the table.

After a few bites, I continue the discussion.

"When you think about Dad today, what comes to mind? Do you have a particular memory that stands out?" My youngest brother, usually the most reticent, speaks up first.

"Nothing in particular because he's everywhere. In everything. All the time. When I fix something around the house. When I watch a soccer game. When I play tennis. When I read the sports pages. Whenever I hear a new song, the first person I want to tell about it is him."

"What do you remember about him?"

"His laughter and his good humor. Dad was larger than life."

"What's your strongest memory?"

"The last concert we saw together. He was in tears by the end of the first song. It was really something. I'd never seen him cry before."

"Was he already ill?"

"Yes. It was shortly before his surgery."

"And what do you feel he has passed on to you?"

"His anxiety. Everything stresses me out. I hope I don't get cancer like he did."

"Don't forget his cancer wasn't genetic," I say.

"Oh, right, I forgot. See how my mind works? I skipped over that good news."

"Don't worry," my other brother jokes. "There are plenty of other cancers."

I turn to him.

"How about you? What was your relationship with Dad like?"

"Great."

"What impression did he leave you with?"

"He was a good man."

He does not elaborate.

"Is that all you have to say?"

"Yes."

Not much of a talker. Like his father. I insist.

"No memory from his final days?"

"Pretty much. The only thing I remember is that you killed him."

All four of us burst out laughing. More precisely, we shed tears of laughter. And it's our father who gives us this laughter. Suddenly, there are five of us at the table again.

III

often attended as a family. It's a bareback horse race held each summer in a public square shaped like a shell. In the days leading up to the race, representatives from each competing *contrade* parades through their tiny neighborhood streets with their horse and head to the local church for a blessing by the priest. Afterward they set up huge tables throughout the city to share pasta and wine while singing local songs. The tension and excitement rise steadily leading up to the race. Packed under the beating sun, thousands of people hold their breath. When the cannon finally fires to start the race, the crowd goes wild. The three laps take less than two minutes, punctuated by the shouts of the crowd crammed into the square and clustered in the windows of the houses along the route. Supporters pounce on the winning horse the moment it crosses the finish line. The celebration lasts until dawn. The last time I was in Siena, I sat at an outdoor café overlooking the main square, opposite the Duomo. I instantly pictured my father. The festivities concentrated everything he enjoyed most in life: food, music, and competition. For the duration of the event, he would eat too much, drink too much, and drive too fast. Yet he was invincible, protected by the wide-eyed Madonna, the Virgin who overlooks and protects the city. My father should have lived here, in this region halfway between North Africa and France, in a fortified city on its cypress-covered hills, on its sun-drenched plains carpeted with olive trees. This is the language he should have spoken, the food he should have eaten, the music he should have listened to. He was at home in this place. But my father was not an adventurer, nor a traveler. He needed his structure. He was a creature of habit. He sought a point to which he could anchor himself. He'd found it in Paris, with my mother. He wouldn't have upset that balance for anything in the world.

*

I sit down at my mother's desk and dial the number of the association. A kind woman asks me to explain our situation. I tell her about my father's illness and its evolution, his fear of death, the denial he's been living in. I explain our concern that hearing the term "palliative care" will send him into a panic.

She says that my father's situation is not out of the ordinary. Generally speaking, the sooner she can talk to patients, the more easily she can calm their anxieties. She asks them about their relationship to dying, what they absolutely want to avoid, such as hospitalization, suffering, being unable to breathe. They often speak freely because their days are not numbered yet. I explain how my father's illness caught us off guard. We didn't have time to ask him these sorts of questions. At that point, it was too late. My father refused to acknowledge his own death. And this ignorance now seems fundamental to sparing him psychological suffering. She never announces on a first meeting that she is part of a palliative-care team because not every patient is capable of calmly addressing their own death. Most are unable to discuss or can only briefly touch on it.

"Death is like the sun, you can't look directly at it for very long," she says. "Most patients hope for a miracle until the very end."

I ask when she thinks she can visit my father.

She must first evaluate the urgency of the situation. To be treated by the association, the patient must be in the terminal phase of illness, the end must be imminent, and the person must be completely dependent, bedridden, unable to get up or feed themselves normally. I confirm that this is the case with my father. She adds that the family's presence is indispensable for an at-home care program. He'll need caregivers.

"We're here," I say. "Day and night. My mother, brothers, and I."

"We'll need to meet with his doctor to get the ball rolling. Your father must be under a doctor's care."

"Yes. Our family doctor."

"Perfect."

"We'll outline a protocol with him to ensure your father suffers as little as possible. Our actions will be gradual. At first, we'll focus on observation. A physical therapist, nurse visits. As your father's state evolves, we'll introduce medical support. At a certain point, we'll administer morphine depending on his degree of pain, in order to reach the maximum level of comfort."

I feel a glimmer of hope. We've found the solution. My father and his lucky star. *Baraka*, he liked to call it. My father was always able to twist the hand of fate. For as long as I can remember, our parents always told us not to give up, to force our luck. The planets seem to be aligning once more.

"The problem," she continues, "is that we are understaffed. It will be hard to get something set up right away. Figure at least a week to organize the coordination meeting between the doctor, nurse, and physical therapist."

"A week? My father will likely be dead by then."

She apologizes. She explains how they have a small staff and are stretched thin; they don't have enough volunteers to respond to the great volume of urgent demands.

"Yet you can consider yourself lucky," she adds. "You live in Paris."

*

I go back to the bedroom. My father is asleep.

I hear my brothers and mother talking in the kitchen, followed by a burst of laughter. A sound that is increasingly rare in the house.

I take advantage of the time alone with my father to lean close and whisper in his ear.

"Dad, please hold on another week." Maybe he hears me. From far away.

I think of the time when my daughter, still an infant, woke us up several times a night. I see myself telling her sternly, with all the seriousness I could muster, "You must let my wife sleep now." Generally, she would cry even harder. I hope my father will be more receptive.

AGONY

Saturday night. I'm on duty. My brothers are enjoying their evening. One is in the country for the weekend, the other at a cousin's birthday party. My mother is also out. Some friends invited her to a play "to take her mind off things." She was hesitant to go but I encouraged her. I find myself alone with my father. He lies before me, motionless, corpselike.

An hour goes by, punctuated by his labored, irregular breathing. From time to time, he becomes restless in his sleep. I step in close and hold his hand to calm him. It's cold. What does that mean? Is it the beginning of the end? Is he going to die tonight?
Many people have described experiences of loved ones hanging on until they were alone. My paternal grandmother, for instance. Though my aunt never left her side, day and night for two months, my grandmother waited for her to slip out to take a shower to pass away.

My father is half asleep. He struggles for air. I get out of my chair, tiptoe across the room, and hide in a corner where he can't see me. If my father wants to let go, now is the time. I give him free rein.
I stand there motionless for a few minutes, holding my breath.
What a relief to imagine him going now, in his sleep.
How liberating. For him. For us.
I creep over to the bed. He hasn't moved.
Still alive.
He's hanging on. Eyes shut.
Mouth open.
Every inhale is a struggle. Each exhale, a fight.

Where would we be if the doctor had accepted our request? That was three days ago. Would he already have taken measures? Would my father

be at peace by now?
I'd like to tell myself I'm happy he's still here. But I can't.

*

I sit in the armchair next to the bed. I can't read, nor do I feel like listening to music. I'm powerless, helpless; I serve no purpose. Outside, it's dark. How much time has passed? I don't know. The only thing I do know: there is no hope. If we could at least fight, try to change the course of events. But no, all we can do is wait. For what? For him to stop breathing once and for all? To suffer enough to be accompanied? "Accompany" is the term the doctor used. "Don't worry, when the time comes, I'll accompany him," he said when we last spoke. What does that mean? Concretely speaking? We need to know. We have the right to know. The uncertainty is unbearable.
Suddenly, a cry. Of pain.
Harrowing.
My father clutches his chest.
Is it cardiac arrest? A freeing heart attack? Then an uncontrollable coughing fit.
He starts to gasp and choke. Like a severe asthma attack. Terrifying.
I try to calm him with one hand. Grab my phone with the other.
I call our doctor.
He doesn't answer.
My father is suffocating before my very eyes. I call an ambulance.
Answering machine.
"You've reached Emergency Services. Your call will be answered shortly. We inform you that this call may be recorded . . ."
Jazz music.
My father is dying.
"Be prepared to give your phone number, first and last name, address, and the nature of your emergency."

Jazz music.

My father grasps at his chest with both hands. He winces in terrible pain. I grab a painkiller on the nightstand and try to get him to swallow it. He throws it up immediately and chokes again.

Jazz music. "Emergency, hello."

"My father can't breathe. Come quick." "What address?"

I give him the address, door code, floor.

"A team is on their way but I need more information so they can best help your father. Why is he having trouble breathing? An accident? Is he ill?"

"He has pancreatic cancer." "What stage?"

"What do you mean?" "Early or terminal?"

I step away from the bed and whisper, "Terminal."

*

Fifteen minutes later, two paramedics and a doctor enter the room. Everything goes very fast. They swoop in on my father. They put him on oxygen.

As the paramedics lift him onto the stretcher, I ask the doctor what's going on.

"Your father is showing signs of respiratory distress," he explains. "His suffering is too great. We're taking him to the hospital to provide some relief, put him on antibiotics, and monitor him for a few days."

"Will he be able to return home?"

"Maybe. Once he's stabilized."

They whisk him away. I walk beside the stretcher. I hold my father's hand. We cross the lobby of the building. Neighbors watch us pass. One of them wishes me luck.

We reach the ambulance. I ask if I can ride along but they refuse. I need to get to the hospital on my own. They close the doors and speed away.

I find myself alone in the middle of the street. I call my mother. No answer. She's probably in the middle of Act II. I alert my brothers. I tell them to meet me at the hospital and head to the taxi stand.

I'm relieved. My father can finally breathe. I don't want him to die anymore. Not right away at least. I want to see him. Hold him in my arms. Alive.

*

My mother and two brothers join me in the intensive-care room where my father has been transferred. We spend the night at his bedside. He sleeps. We don't. His breathing is much easier.

*

In the morning, as we're trying to dole out shifts at my father's bedside, a doctor enters the room.

My father is in a stupor. His eyes open. When the doctor questions him, he replies by slightly moving his head. The doctor turns to us. He explains that my father is having difficulty breathing because the cancer has spread to his lungs. He suggests we find a spot in palliative care. My mother tries to step in, but not soon enough. My father grows agitated. He knows. It's the word he's feared for months. "Palliative." Now there is no doubt. No remedy. No hope. He is going to die.

His breathing quickens. He starts to sweat. His body stiffens. His heart starts pounding. He clumsily yanks the oxygen tube from his nose. Starts gasping for breath again. He fixes his gaze on a point in the distance, straight ahead. The doctor calls to a nurse out in the corridor. "Panic attack," he snaps. "Diazepam."

A young woman bursts in with a syringe. She gives my father the shot.

My mother is at his side, stroking his cheek, whispering reassuring words into his ear. He gradually calms down and then begins to cry. He sobs with his hands cupped over his mouth.

When was the last time my father cried? I have no memory of it. Maybe

he never has in front of us. How did we end up here?
I turn to my brothers and suggest we step out.

We take the elevator down to the cafeteria. Two interns are talking. "I've had it with this wing," one of them says. "I'm sick of watching people die. It never stops."

*

Back up on my father's floor, our mother is out in the corridor talking to the doctor. She is furious. She chastises him for his blunder. She demands to take my father back home.
The doctor apologizes and argues. It's too soon. He plans to administer small doses of morphine to ease the pain. He wants to see how my father reacts. He'd like to keep him the night for observation, after which perhaps he can return home the next day.
My mother gives in. It will give us time to get organized.

*

After 36 hours in the hospital, my father is back home the following day. The journey in the ambulance goes well. He arrives in a wheelchair with an oxygen tube, a little tank hooked onto the chair.
Our family doctor is there to welcome him. With the paramedic's assistance, he helps my father back into his bed.
He tells us that the hospital began injecting morphine. With no side effects. A nurse will come by regularly to evaluate my father's level of pain. She'll give him injections if needed and add anxiolytics to keep him calm. The doctor explains that we just passed a critical stage, upsetting for everyone, but the situation should stabilize within a few days.
He also tells us he will stop feeding my father through the drip. From now on, he'll get a hydrating solution only.

"Won't he starve to death?" my mother worries.
The doctor reassures her. A terminally ill patient has no appetite. They don't feel hunger.

*

I call the palliative-care association. They tell me they've accepted my father, and the coordination meeting is scheduled for the end of the week. Early the following week at the latest.

*

Since he learned his days were numbered, my father's attitude has changed. He's gone totally silent. Sleeps most of the time. When he's awake, his eyes are vacant.
We no longer interact.

*

His state worsens by the day.
He grows thinner, increasingly yellow and lifeless. As if he's given up.
Long hours during which nothing happens. He wheezes, moans, fidgets. Smells bad.
My mother lights candles.
He has trouble breathing. There's phlegm in his throat.
My brother takes his hand. It hurts. He groans and pushes him away. Pain makes him aggressive.
His mouth is dry. His lips chapped.
He coughs. When we try to get him to drink, he spits the liquid out. We spray his mouth with a mineral water atomizer. It seems to help. But he says nothing.
It's harder and harder for him to talk, and he does so less and less, with

increasing incoherence. We listen closely to everything he says, on alert for a message or revelation, something remarkable or memorable.

*

We push degradation onto you until the end. You lose your dignity.
You, who were so handsome and proud.
I would like to not see you anymore. I would like what we're going through today to not spoil everything we've shared up until now.

*

My mother asks the doctor.
"Why is it lasting so long when we know it's over?"
"I'm here to relieve his suffering, but I can't do more than that."
She lets out a sob. The doctor hugs her. If even he, whom she has known for forty years, won't help, there's truly nothing anyone can do.

*

Since our father came back from the hospital, we've been at his bedside 24/7. Helpless witnesses to his descent into hell.
He grows increasingly congested each day. He gasps.
His breathing is more and more chaotic.
As soon as he shuts his eyes, he falls asleep. No longer responds. Doesn't react when we touch him. It's like he's dead. But still in pain.

DEATH

Saturday morning. It's been one week since my father nearly suffocated. Seven days of torture. Seven days of decline. Seven days of tears. Seven days of guilt. Seven days that destroyed everything. Seven days that will haunt us for the rest of our lives.

Why didn't I let him die last weekend rather than call an ambulance? I wish I'd been cold-blooded enough. But I couldn't do it.

*

The family doctor stops by to see my father in the morning. He tells us his daughter is getting married that weekend. A nurse will replace him. She'll come by every six hours to give my father a morphine shot. Monday, when the doctor is back, he'll install a pump to make the process more comfortable.

"It should all go fine," he says. "Your father will sleep a lot. If there's the slightest complication, call me. I'll talk you through it over the phone."

He leaves.

*

We gear up for another weekend of gasping and suffering. The hours at my father's bedside are so trying that we've decided to take turns. My mother, brothers, and I each do a four-hour shift every twelve hours.

*

I use my first free afternoon to watch my son play soccer. We had recently registered him for a local soccer club. Today is his first official game. I take him to the stadium where he joins his teammates. When he emerges from the locker room in his brand-new uniform, he winks at me and heads to the field. He would have loved his grandfather to see his debut as goalie.

At halftime, as I give him advice about the best technique to free up the ball, my phone rings.

It's my mother.

My father is in severe pain and once again fighting for breath, despite his oxygen being set to the maximum. She needs help.

I hug my son and hurry out of the stadium.

When I reach my parents' home, my mother tells me the nurse has just given my father an injection of morphine. Things have settled down. The nurse will come back in four hours.

I find my father lying in his bed with his eyes closed. My mother and I sit at his bedside. She takes my hand. We sit there a long time, side by side. The room is filled with my father's rales, rhythmic and loud, like nails scratching on a chalkboard.

*

After two hours, he's moaning again. My father's face is twisted in a grimace of pain.

The nurse hurries back earlier than planned. She's fine with anticipating a little, but warns us: she can't exceed six milligrams per 24 hours, the dose indicated on the prescription. This will be the last injection of the day. She won't be able to give him another morphine shot until the next morning. But, by the looks of things, that will hardly suffice. She's sorry, but only a doctor can write a new prescription.

I try to contact ours but he doesn't answer. He must be at the church, at city hall, or already on the dance floor.

I call Emergency Services. They are slammed but promise to send someone as soon as possible.

*

My mother can't bear the thought of standing helplessly by while my father suffers. She heads to the nearest pharmacy intending to get whatever it takes to relieve his pain. She explains that her husband is dying and asks if they can make an exception, this one time. The pharmacist, whom she's known for years, is very apologetic but is unable to grant her request. She explains that morphine doses are strictly controlled, each vial is numbered, and only a written prescription on security paper can procure the precious substance.

*

Violent coughing fit.
My father says "ouch," closes his eyes, doesn't move, falls asleep.
I have no idea how the coming minutes are going to play out. The coming hours. I have no idea how my father is going to die. But I can tell he's reached the end. If he doesn't wake back up, his last word will be "ouch." It's terrible. I think about waking him up. I want him to say something else, anything at all, but not that.
His rales are more and more distressing. His body twitches in his sleep.
His eyes suddenly snap open.
He stares at me. Begging me to put an end to this.
Calling for help.
I sit there paralyzed before him, disarmed.
I've often imagined placing a cushion over his face and pressing down. Like in that film where Jean-Louis Trintignant can no longer stand by idly as his wife suffers and smothers her with a pillow. The film is called *Love*. Because that is indeed what it comes down to. An act of love. Why turn lovers into killers? Why can't we enjoy the freedom to die as we enjoy our freedom to live? We should have the right to bring relief to our fathers, mothers, brothers, sisters, and children without being considered murderers.

My father says "ouch" again. He tries to catch his breath. Can't.
A deep, raspy death rattle emerges from his throat. It gets stuck.
He winces. Everything stops. His eyes are open.
The rales have stopped. He's stopped moving. Stopped breathing.
His face is pale. His cheeks hollow.
His mouth open.
The mouth that will never laugh again.
I almost touch it.
Then, gently, like in a movie, I lift his wrist and place my thumb on his inner forearm to take his pulse. The vein no longer beats. Nor does his heart. Probably.
I am in shock.
My mother still isn't back from the pharmacy. I need to tell her.
Before she gets back, I want to erase any evidence of suffering from my father's face, smooth his cheeks to relax his features, close his mouth.
Is his skin already cold? I don't dare touch it.
I don't want my mother to see him like this, but I'm paralyzed.
I can't tear my eyes from him.
I already regret this image. The ugly grimace of pain on my father's beautiful face.
The father I loved so much.
I think: so this is what dying according to the rules is like. I'm relieved that neither my mother nor my brothers saw this. Just like I was the only one in South Africa who knew, I'll keep this image to myself. I won't speak of it. Ever. I make a vow.
Too late.
My mother walks in.
She ventures over slowly. She knows.
She strokes his face.
She tries to close his mouth. But his jaw falls back open.
"How horrible," she says. "We can't leave him like this."

She disappears into the bathroom and returns with a scarf. She lifts his chin, wraps the scarf around his head, and ties it in a knot on top.

*

A half hour later, the doorbell rings. It's the doctor from the emergency medical service. He apologizes for being late and records our father's death. Meanwhile, my brothers have arrived.

The youngest has already called the funeral home. My mother doesn't want my father to stay in the house. She wants his body taken away as quickly as possible. She's horrified by the idea of a wake.

*

Only the closest family members are contacted. My wife, my brothers' wives, and my father's sister. His brother doesn't want to come.

Everyone takes a turn at my father's bedside. They pay their last respects and join my mother where she has retreated, in the living room.

The undertaker has already arrived. He stands off in a corner of the room. Waiting to begin washing and laying out the body. His presence disturbs me. The thought of this stranger soon handling my father, disinfecting his body, sealing his orifices, injecting formalin into his arteries is unbearable. I never expected to have any contact with this man. I thought this kind of thing happened much later. But my mother decided otherwise.

The body will be prepared during the night and removed early in the morning. The cremation is scheduled for two days later.

*

We leave the house one after another. My youngest brother stays to keep

our mother company. They'll sleep in the room adjacent to my parents'. In twin beds.
My brother goes to bed. He weeps quietly while my mother removes her makeup in the bathroom. She slips into a bathrobe and goes into the room with the corpse. My father lies on his back. His ghostlike body is draped in a sheet. Alone in the dark. The undertaker has gone. My mother approaches and observes him silently. She calls to my brother in the next room.

"Come see, he's peaceful at last." My brother says he'd rather not.
My mother stands motionless at the foot of the bed a long while. She takes advantage of these final moments beside her husband, forcing herself not to think of the abyss that has opened up before her.

AFTER

The next day, my brothers and I meet at my mother's house at dawn. Her house, from now on.
Earl Grey tea, fresh-squeezed orange juice, toast, homemade raspberry jam. The same breakfast for forty years. In the summer, we picked wild berries along the roads and our mother cooked them in a big copper cauldron that smelled like stewed fruit and sugar. Those were the days of putting firecrackers in cow patties, catching crayfish, eating stuffed cabbage in the village, watching tennis matches. A father and three sons. Perfect for playing doubles.

We watch as the body is taken away. Two men walk past in the hallway. With outstretched arms, they carry the shrouded corpse of our father. They leave the house.

My mother wants to leave, too. The news of my father's death has begun to spread. The phone starts ringing. She doesn't answer. Doesn't want to speak to anyone. Doesn't want to see anyone. All she wants to do is get away, as fast as possible. She knows friends and family will begin arriving soon. She must flee. So she won't have to justify herself. Why did you remove the body so quickly? Why didn't you let us see him one last time? Why didn't you allow us to say our goodbyes? Why cremation? The thought of her house filled with grieving, weeping faces fills her with horror.
Her ferocity is in proportion to her pain.
At that moment, she has no compassion left. Neither for friends, nor for family. People she loves but to whom she doesn't want to answer. Her sorrow is overwhelming. She can't bear having to put on a brave face. She knows she'll be reproached for taking charge and making all the decisions surrounding his death. But she doesn't care. It's her husband. She does

what she wants.
"And anyone who doesn't understand, they can just deal with it. Come on, boys."
She wants to walk in the forest with her sons. We drive to the woods in my brother's car.

*

A friend takes over at the house. She will greet visitors. Explain the situation to them: the body is already gone, and so is the family.
The first person to arrive is an aunt from Tunisia. When she learns the house is empty and the cremation already scheduled, she loses her temper. That's not how you treat the deceased! A death is sacred. It must be commemorated. It takes time for the soul to leave its terrestrial shell. One must treat the dead as the living. We must not touch the corpse. We must pray for the departed. We undress the body. Drape it in a white sheet. Lay it on the floor. Place a candle alongside the face. We rip a hole in our clothes over the heart to express our heartbreak at the loss. We don't burn a dead body. Cremation is a violation of its integrity.
At the time, I naively believed that what shocked Jews about cremation had something to do with the crematoria of concentration camps. Later, I discovered that interment is a sacred act, obligatory according to the Torah; not burying the body meant depriving the soul of eternal rest.
"Why doesn't she answer her phone?" the aunt fumes before storming off.
Next comes a group of men. Childhood friends from Tunis. They are also shocked to learn the body is no longer there. Filled with sorrow. One of them suggests calling the person in charge of the funeral arrangements. An old acquaintance who has handled family burials for years. They want to pay their last respects to their friend. The four of them head to the cemetery. When they arrive, they are led to the morgue. An employee slides my father out of the refrigerated compartment. They have ten minutes to mourn at his side in the cold room.

*

We walk through the forest. It's the first day of autumn and the leaves are starting to turn yellow. We are silent. Unable to wrap our minds around what has happened. Yesterday we were complete. A mother, a father, and three sons. Today, one of our limbs has been amputated. A family is a perfectly balanced mobile. When one part is lost, the entire structure is thrown off. How are we supposed to live now? And my mother? How will she come back from such a loss? Her lifelong mate. Fifty-three years of living and loving together. Working together. A constant connection. He was her love, husband, best friend, partner, alter ego. My mother's existence orbited my father's. And vice versa. She will have to learn to walk on one leg. As I write these lines, I know she managed to reinvent herself. She managed to build a new life, a different one. But on that day, as our feet crunch over dead leaves on the forest floor, I am worried. I put my arm around her shoulders. She rests her head against my cheek.

It's a beautiful late morning. The sun filters through the leaves. We continue walking through the trees. The forest is filled with hikers and Sunday joggers. My mother's phone keeps vibrating in her coat pocket. She sits down on a bench in the shade to answer her sister's call.

I walk over to a pond. My brothers follow.

"He was so young," one of them murmurs.

"No," I say. "Sixty-nine isn't young. To die at 25 is young. He lived a whole life. A wonderful life."

My phone rings. The number of the palliative-care association appears on my screen. I'm about to refuse the call but then decide to pick up.

"Hello?"

"Hello. We're calling about your father. I have good news: the coordination meeting was held this morning. Which means we care for your father starting this afternoon."

"My father died last night."

We sit down at an outdoor table at a restaurant on the edge of the forest. We order a bottle of wine and wait silently for the waiter to bring it. He pours the wine and tells us to "enjoy." We raise our glasses joylessly.

"To *Nonno*."

"*Nonno*" is "grandpa" in Italian. The nickname my father gave himself when his grandchildren were born.

"I'm angry," my mother says. "It can't be possible to die like that in the 21st century. If we were able to do what we'd wanted, your father would have gone sooner, with no suffering. Instead, he had a horrible end. . . . Boys, I'm counting on you to spare me that."

My brothers and I, in unison: "We promise, Mom."

ACKNOWLEDGMENTS

My mother,

My brothers,

Éléonore Pourriat, for her support and her help, always,
Alban Guitteny, my old accomplice,
Michel Aronovicz, for all of his essential advice,

Alix Penent, my French publisher, and Soizic Molkhou, without whom this book would not be this book,

Charlotte Pailleux, for the end.

Also,
Christophe André, Isabelle Baumgaertner, Augustin Boulanger, Florence Bourg, Thomas Chabrol, Daniel Cherqui, Jenifer Clergeot, Martine Cohen, Pascale Favre, Claire Fourcade, Mitty Gain, Julie Pouillon, Jean-Louis Pourriat, Vincent Silvan, Dorothée Werner, Jean-Luc Audy, Antoine Bing, Irène Cohen, Philomène Cohen, Clémentine Deroudille, Julien Guérif, François Leininger, Bertrand Mouly, Antoine Novat, Virginie Person, Matthieu Prada, Maëlle Sagnes, Lou Svahn, and Marie-Lorna Vaconsin.

And for the English-language version, Suzanne Slesin, Frederico Farina, and Julian Cosma. Thank you for your loyalty.

BIOGRAPHY

BENOIT COHEN

Born in 1969, Benoit Cohen is a French filmmaker, screenwriter, and writer. After studying architecture in Paris, he studied filmmaking at New York University. When he returned to France, after producing several short films, he directed his first feature film *Chameleone* in 1996. Between 2000 and 2014, Cohen made five other feature films including *Our Precious Children* and *If You Love Me, Follow Me*, as well as a few documentaries and three television series.

In 2014, after moving to Brooklyn, New York, Cohen drove a taxicab for several months to gain perspective for a screenplay about a French actress who wanted to become a taxi driver in New York. He wrote *Yellow Cab*, a book about this experience, followed by *Mohammad, My Mother and Me*, the story of his mother and the Afghan refugee she hosted in her home for two years, which became the movie *My Motherland* in 2023.

Publisher / Editorial Director: Suzanne Slesin
Creative Director: Frederico Farina
Assistant Editor: Julian Cosma
Copy Editor: Amelia Kutschbach
ISBN: 978-1-938461-70-5
Library of Congress: 2025935166
First Edition
Printed in Spain

Original French edition of *Formidable* ©Flammarion, Paris, 2023
Translated from the French by Michelle Noteboom

Pointed Leaf Press, LLC. 136 Baxter Street, Suite 1C, New York, NY 10013.